A PURELY WRONG STORY

ESCAPING SEXUAL SHAME, EXPOSING A GAME-CHANGER, AND EDITING YOUR LIFE STORY WITHOUT CHANGING THE FACTS

LAUREL BURNS

AUTHOR ACADEMY elite

Published by Author Academy Elite
PO Box 43, Powell, OH 43065
www.AuthorAcademyElite.com

Identifiers:
LCCN: 2023914232
ISBN: 979-8-88583-242-7 (paperback)
ISBN: 979-8-88583-243-4 (hardback)
ISBN: 979-8-88583-244-1 (ebook)
Available in paperback, hardback, e-book, and audiobook

Manuscript:
All Scripture quotations, unless otherwise indicated, are taken from the Holy Bible, New International Version®, NIV®. Copyright © 1973, 1978, 1984, 2011 by Biblica, Inc.™ Used by permission of Zondervan. All rights reserved worldwide. All rights reserved worldwide. www.zondervan.com The "NIV" and "New International Version" are trademarks registered in the United States Patent and Trademark Office by Biblica, Inc.™

Scripture quotations marked MSG are taken from The Message, copyright © 1993, 2002, 2018 by Eugene H. Peterson. Used by permission of NavPress. All rights reserved. Represented by Tyndale House Publishers.

Scripture quotations marked (NLT) are taken from the *Holy Bible*, New Living Translation, copyright © 1996, 2004, 2015 by Tyndale House Foundation. Used by permission of Tyndale House Publishers, Carol Stream, Illinois 60188. All rights reserved.

Scripture Snippets:
All Scripture quotations are taken from *The Message*, copyright © 1993, 2002, 2018 by Eugene H. Peterson. Used by permission of NavPress. . All rights reserved. Represented by Tyndale House Publishers.

This book deals with sexual abuse. While the author has taken great lengths to deal with the subject matter compassionately and respectfully, it may be troubling for some readers. Discretion is advised. The information in this book is accurate and complete to the best of the author's knowledge. Any advice or recommendations are without guarantee by the author or publisher. Neither the publisher nor the author shall be held liable or responsible for any loss or damage allegedly arising from any suggestion or information contained in this book.

Alyssa, Madison, and Faith, it is my joy to dedicate this book to you, but my most incredible honor and privilege is simply being your mom. You girls are my favorite parts in my life story, and I love each of you more with every passing day.

TABLE OF CONTENTS

INTRODUCTION

As I entertained the idea of writing a book about shame from sexual experiences, a rare incident occurred in South Africa during a surfing competition. Mick Fanning, an Australian professional surfer, first felt a pull on his leg rope. He had been floating on his surfboard, awaiting his turn, when he spied the circling fin. Mick's instinct immediately took over, and he swam as hard as he could in a frantic attempt to reach shore while still surveying the waters. A video captured the suspense as a shark surfaced behind Mick's view and violently knocked him into the water. For a moment, it seemed that may be the end of Mick Fanning. Yet, since the attack happened during a surfing competition, nearby officials rushed to Mick's rescue. Pulling him out of the water and into the safety of their boat, the officials found Mick shaken from the shark but, ultimately, unharmed.

In an interview after the attack, Mick said, "I was just waiting for teeth."[1]

His memory resonated with me, for I have felt teeth before. As I aimlessly drifted—clueless—a hidden enemy circled, intimidated, and attacked me physically and emotionally. This enemy's teeth sank in, leaving me wounded and bleeding for years.

Flailing against the currents of life, I grasped and kicked to no avail. Until, by the grace of God, a lifeboat arrived.

It pulled my exhausted body from the waters into its solid protection and carried me to rescue.

I can see other girls and women still in the ocean of life. Some are leisurely bobbing, unaware of the infested waters. Others are exhausted from swimming and barely treading water.

I do not know your exact story, but I know that you are barely hanging on. You are caught in an enemy's grip and tangled in circumstances that have plagued the earth since the beginning of time—an epidemic proportionate only to the vastness of the ocean.

I know you are out there.

You may be floating all alone, while no one else even notices. But I can see you. Now, try to imagine me as well. The faint glow of my rescue light precedes me. Slowly, my boat's form becomes discernible. The light grows brighter. I am on my way. I have a life preserver to throw you, one that can bring you to the only true safety zone. Please don't swim away. Please hear me out.

You assume you will have to imagine my voice as well. Yet you will recognize it when you hear it, for I will not speak my own words. Instead, I will speak for the One who sent me to:

> Bind up the brokenhearted, to proclaim freedom for the captives and release from darkness for the prisoners, to proclaim the year of the Lord's favor and the day of vengeance of our God, to comfort all who mourn, and provide for those who grieve in Zion—to bestow on them a crown of beauty instead of ashes, the oil of joy instead of mourning, and a garment of praise instead of a spirit of despair.
>
> Isaiah 61:1b-3a

You have heard that voice deep down in your heart and mind, whispering, "There's a better way."

Please, grab hold.

PART 1

THE BEGINNING CHAPTERS

1

CALLING IT

If I asked you to define "sex," what definition would you give? Without hesitation, I can say that as a child, I possessed a particularly negative view of sex. I would have described it as "the gross act I saw on television" or "the reason my parents disappeared sometimes and left me alone." As I grew older, different vulgar occasions and sights further bombarded my senses and memories of sex.

I have come to realize that, as children, we lack the ability to control our surroundings. Our helplessness forces us to depend on the adults in our lives. Innocent and impressionable, we soak in the actions and experiences we encounter. Then, with the depths of our childhood wisdom, we try to unify our experiences in a way that logically connects all the pieces. Without knowing, we form our foundational beliefs about life and, specifically, our beliefs about sex.

I do not know where your thoughts or definition of sex might lean today. However, chances are, you, too, might have lacked high regard for the word. I did not have a family who would openly discuss sex—or even boys—with me. As a helpless child, I floundered to define what the world had thrust before me. Truth be told, it took me decades to wrestle with my definition as I went down some agonizing and lonely roads.

While not identical, we all bring life stories and experiences that can share a common thread, especially when considering detrimental sexual experiences. Even though the aftermaths of our experiences may not spin off in the same direction, prevailing tendencies often remain. Priceless understanding results if you find someone who has walked in your shoes. Someone who relates to the feelings you may have previously kept hidden. A relationship clicks, and you forge an immediate, unspoken bond. But profound, haunting loneliness will likely settle in if you cannot connect with someone else. I know because I spent most of my life in that state of loneliness. Yet, loneliness presents a dangerously fertile ground for the seed of shame to begin its rampant growth. Shame sneers, "What has happened? What have you done? You have thrown your life away. Look at it—shattered and ruined. No one else comes close to being as bad as you. From now on, you'll have to hide what you have chosen to do or hide what others have done to you. You can't let anyone else know what has unraveled in your life because they could never understand. Accept it: You will never be the same as everyone else."

The only way to break hidden shame's isolating feeling is through connection, and connection always begins with a story.

MY STORY

My story begins, oddly enough, on a high note with a friend. A best friend. And though the calendar indicates that decades have passed since this high point in my life, my heart can evoke the time's powerful emotions with such ease that it's liable to tell you my high note faded only yesterday.

I attended small private schools throughout my schooling, and because of the smaller class sizes, I experienced few friends. Yet, with time, I was able to form one close bond with a girl classmate. Her friendship became everything to me. Every weekend, my friend and I were inseparable. We spent the night at each other's house, went out, or talked on the phone. Even her parents made a mark on my life; they treated me like a daughter and allowed me to join their family vacations.

Sometimes I had to pinch myself, but this was how it was for years of my middle and high school life. I finally had someone in my life who noticed me. I finally had someone who knew me and cared about me. I felt loved, and I could not have been happier. My life had morphed into a blissful dream.

Until. Until one day, a switch went off, and my friend shut me out. She stopped talking to me. Stopped calling. Stopped even making eye contact. We had resolved a few arguments in our friendship before, so at first, I figured things would blow over. But the silence continued for several days. I wrote a long, heartfelt letter to her, apologizing for whatever I did to upset her to this extent. She responded with a short note saying, "Thank you for the letter." Nevertheless, we were never friends again, and I have yet to solve the mystery of why my dear friend cut off our friendship.

Though I was baffled by the "whys" of my loss, I was well acquainted with the "hows." How I never felt more alone. How I now had no one to talk to or call. No one to hang out with. From nowhere, a barreling train of despair had plowed into me and derailed my happy life. My world came to a screeching halt. Hours and days passed, filled with my sobbing prayers, "Please, God, help me. Help me not to feel so alone!"

So my countless prayers appeared answered when *he* walked into my life. He seemed to be the only person to acknowledge my existence. He came around to hang out or called to talk on the phone at night. Either way, laughter always ensued. We shared similar interests and personalities. I met his family. Forget admiration—I idolized him. Intelligent and athletic, he was the perfect fit for the void in my world, and he grew to be my new best friend.

I never really dated in high school. We can blame it on the small private school again, shall we? Although, I didn't have a fear of interacting with guys. In fact, I had always enjoyed having guy friends for as long as I could remember. In my experience, guys just operated on a more easygoing and less dramatic level than my girl friends. So this new guy did not count as my first guy friend, yet he was only that—a guy *friend*. Sure, others would have considered him good-looking, but I was not interested in him for his looks. To me, we bonded for genuine reasons. And without involving romantic feelings, our friendship didn't have to grapple with any interference or complications.

Or so I thought.

He had come over to my house. Nothing unusual. But, at some point, he shifted the conversation and began to talk about sex—not a regular topic of discussion for us. He asked me if I was a virgin. "Yes, of course," I answered. To my relief, he dropped the awkward subject, and the otherwise ordinary night continued until, without warning, he leaned over to kiss me! I pulled away, taken aback and confused. He tried to convince me that friends often kiss, but he could not persuade me. Although I attempted to avoid his repeated advances, it did not deter him.

I do not know if you have ever had an out-of-body experience. Who knows if that accurately explains what I felt that night? Perhaps shock alone had seized me and caused me to feel removed from the situation and paralyzed to escape it. Yet, before I knew it, I was naked. Naked. With a boy. Who was also naked. *Not* normal.

His advances intensified beyond my strength, and I didn't know how to respond. I have often thought, *Why didn't I scream?* But, at the time, the idea of being found naked by my parents made that option seem impossible. With his weight on top of me, pain jarred me out of any possible out-of-body, disconnected state. Though I struggled to free myself and push away the pain, my efforts proved futile.

Culture had trained me to correlate sex with desire and pleasure, but neither of those feelings was present in my experience. So without any other point of reference, no light bulb turned on in my mind, and I was oblivious to the physical act that had taken place. Neither did my innocence understand why my sheets had blood spots, but I concluded that, if nothing else, it supplied evidence to confirm the pain.

He got up from the bed and dressed to leave. Then, as if sensing my confusion, he asked, "So, are you a virgin anymore?" But he didn't bother to wait for a reply.

Instead, chuckling, he walked out of my room and left.

I was left reeling in my bed. *That is what just happened*? But here I was. Naked.

And lonelier than ever before.

MY DEDUCTIONS

And so it began. Another plummet, you could say, but this nose-dive would leave behind catastrophic damage far exceeding the wreckage from losing my girl friend.

I spent most of the next day trying to wrap my mind around my swirling thoughts. Time and again, I bumped into my unyielding indoctrinations that warned: Sex should only happen in marriage, and therefore, only evil, sinful people have sex before marriage.

Standing on the wrong side of purity, I felt like a banner hung over my head for all to see. Exposed, clear as day, everyone could read my banner's label: Bad.

So, alone and broken, I formed my definition of sex. But posing a greater significance, I formed a definition of myself. And from my surroundings, I gathered these pieces:

I must have had sex.

I just did the gross act that I had found so despicable.

I must be loathsome now too.

I cannot go back in time.

I cannot undo anything.

Things are forever changed.

I have forever changed.

I used to be good.

But now, I am bad.

And there's nothing I can do about it.

I am evil; No one would ever count me as good again.

So what does it matter what I do now?

If I have already ruined myself, then why does anything else matter?

And those thoughts shaped the foundation for the succeeding stages of my life. I inferred that I was permanently ruined, damaged, hopeless goods. But the deductions did not stop there. No, with my hot mess mentality, I continued to think.

One fact particularly rattled me: I would have fully trusted this guy before yesterday. Without question, I had considered him a friend—my best friend. So by default, he wouldn't be capable of untrustworthy behavior, right? Otherwise, that wouldn't make any sense, for that would contradict every definition of a best friend that I knew. No, I needed to find the logic in things, and maintaining my hopeful belief in him seemed a much easier pill to swallow. Yes, this rationale even allowed me to continue to have a best friend in my life. So if this is what it took to keep him in my life—if sex kept him in my life—then I knew what I must do.

After all, what do my actions matter? Ruined already, remember?

Guided by the principle that my actions didn't matter, I acted accordingly. For years I handed over my body in exchange for companionship in an attempt to grasp hold of any ounce of togetherness that I could.

MY WALLOW

But, before long, my grasp disintegrated. Perhaps your discernment kicked in sooner than mine, and you saw that one coming. I hope for your sake you did! But you could only call me blindsided as I unraveled signs, bit by bit. I began to learn the other ways he spent his time and with whom he spent his time—that is to say, another girl was in the picture. Other warning signs also emerged. I noticed his tendency to visit unannounced and at odd times—as if I were a last resort when no other options existed. He would never, say, plan a date. When I considered it, it was rare for us to even go out in public together. No, to him, my usefulness boiled down to just one thing.

But while sanity was trying to creep in, my emotions were still trying to erect blockades to maintain the safe world that I thought I had created. The wishful world that soothed, *You can trust him! He is your best friend! A best friend would never hurt you—in this way especially! He believes, like you, that sex is for marriage. Therefore, he must equate you with forever! He must really like you! No, he must love you!*

But as his patterns replayed, I decided to confront him. I only did so to dispel my nagging fears because I refused to believe my suspicions could be justified. Without a blatant admission, I could not accept that he was anything less than I imagined. I could not believe the reality on my own. So I threw my "evidence" at him, but what he threw back rocked me to the core. He agreed with my conclusions! He *was* using me, but somehow the blame was mine because I should have known he could not pull away from the physical nature of our relationship.

While my life has been fraught with poor choice after poor choice, I have never regretted what I did that day. At least in my sane moments.

I walked away from him and out of his life—in both the literal and figurative way. I never spoke to him again, and I closed the door on that chapter.

I wish I could tell you that day began a turning point for me or led to a significant revelation in my life.

But I cannot.

While I had closed one door, I was unaware I had opened another. A new door that somehow led to the old, familiar pain—once again.

Loneliness rushed in and wasted no time taking up residence in my heart. I wallowed in its familiar, shadowed corners.

My choices rendered the evidence for the depth of my wallow. I continued to seek out companionship. With desperation. And at all costs. Men just needed that physical element, apparently. So if I wanted companionship, I was left with no choice.

No surprise, my attempts failed to satisfy me. I began to blame myself for being so stupid and for doing the things I had done, and I found myself more hopeless than ever before.

If only.

If only that night had never happened. Then I would be "fixed." "Good" again. Happy even. If only I had fought longer, pushed harder, or screamed. If only I had said "no" more.

But that thought jolted me and caused reality, at least in part, to dawn.

I *said,* "no."

Many, many times.

Theoretically, only one "no" should have been needed to signify protest.

But I expressed my hesitancy even beyond a vocal objection. Because I did push and I did try to stop the advances.

No longer could I fault my inaction because my actions *were* enough.

At least, they *should* have been enough.

So what did that mean?

That meant I did not ask for nor cause what happened to me.

That meant I was *forced* to do that act.

But if I could not validate the situation as an act by a trustworthy friend, then where did that leave my memories? What *had* happened?

MY CALL

And so I came face-to-face with the first real definition for my experience that I had ever formed up until this point in my life—"date rape."

Perhaps you, too, have come to know this definition firsthand?

I had always assumed that rape implied a faceless act—an intruder, a stranger, the guilty masked individual portrayed on television or in movies. *That* constituted rape. But that didn't depict what happened to me.

My memory had a face and a name.

However, adding the word "date" allows for that precise distinction. The difference implies that this form of rape can occur on a date, but a date by no means encompasses the singular instance or parameter for this experience! Rather, the term applies when you know who has forced you into a sexual act. And, yes, you are forced—against your will or request—to do something you do not want to do. Or forced to do something you do not understand.

You see, my arm could be dangling from its socket. Pain could be coursing through my body. I may even recognize, "Hey, something is off here." But until I call my arm "broken"—call it for what it is—I can never take steps to mend anything. I can never reach healing.

So I share all this to ask, where do you need healing? What has brought you to pick up this book? Where has life broken you?

Now, Your Story

Perhaps you, too, had choices taken from you. Someone robbed pieces of your heart and life.

Perhaps you can relate to my story. A face, a name. A friend. A boyfriend. A family member. Events, stories, and memories that time will not fade.

Maybe you do not have those things. Maybe a stranger did walk into your life and walk out with your whole world. Questions, fears, and blanks linger without closure.

Maybe you have been a victim of sexual trafficking. Others bought opportunities to use your body. They saw you as an item, a piece of property, and demanded financial gain and physical gratification. None regarded your body as your own. Instead, exploitation, humiliation, and degradation were pounded into your very being.

Maybe you were willing to give up pieces of yourself, but it was for all the wrong reasons: fear, insecurity, previous abuse, loneliness, or a desire to please. Perhaps, whatever life threw at you had left you feeling as deluded as I had felt, and you, too, felt hopeless and defenseless against the options it presented. You saw no other way. Compromises, sacrifices, and empty exchanges inflicted emotional bruises and wounds far beyond skin-deep.

Whatever circumstances brought you to this point and this book—my heart breaks for you. No topic is as dear or sensitive as how your body is used sexually. A righteous anger should inflame when anyone falls prey to sexual victimization. *Zero* justification exists to permit, force, or pressure any unwelcome sexual act.

Let me repeat it to ensure you hear me: It is *never* acceptable to be forced or pressured into sexual activity. By anyone. At any time. Under any circumstance. Never. Ever. Did I mention never?

You did nothing to deserve that hateful crime. You could not have stopped it. You could not have prevented it any more than you can prevent cancer. You do not need to blame yourself any longer. We live in a broken world. People, ourselves included, do not always treat others with proper respect. People do not always honor others. People do not always put others before themselves. No, as you know, people can be deceptive and manipulative, employing crippling forces. And others become prey to them—not because they did something wrong, but solely because we all live in a world where evil poses a terrible and real threat.

Maybe you are thinking, "But someone did not take advantage of me. I chose to do those acts." Then let me ask you to consider this scene: two people stand by a table where a lit candle rests.

PERSON #1: (*Picking up the candle and handing it to PERSON #2*) Will you take this candle and burn my hand with it?

If PERSON #2 proceeds to burn PERSON #1, what do you notice about this scenario? Yes, PERSON #1 is asking to have a reckless action performed on her body. Any injury that follows will be a consequence of her request. But does PERSON #2 have no choice in the matter? You bet he does. He could choose to burn PERSON #1 merely because of the opportunity. Or, he could choose to be the voice of reason and refuse to carry out an act that would bring known harm.

We all face choices every day. How we treat others and respond to them—emotionally or physically—all falls squarely on us as individuals. Yet, in sexual encounters, more than one person is always involved. But since we cannot control other people's responses or emotions, we cannot bear the responsibility for their choices.

Therefore, you may need to own the offers you have extended to others, but they are obligated to own their responses.

YOUR CALL

So, where does this leave us?

We all know our stories. Too well, right?

You might think so, and you might think you have it all figured out. But I am asking you to examine your story in a fresh light. Like me, could any skewed perceptions be holding you in hostage chains? Do your previous definitions or thoughts about your story now strike you as questionable?

For me, it required a monumental step to call my situation what it was: date rape.

I know it can be scary to accept the truth. Sometimes denial feels safer. Giving a title to something can, somehow, make it seem more real. And going back through the abyss of our pain often brings a lot of gunk to the surface—painful gunk that is easier to bury, hide, or run away from. I know, I know. But remember me telling you I tried that route? For way too many years, I tried that route. Okay, yes, for too many decades, I tried that route. Pathetic but true. Please do not think you can follow in my footsteps and somehow end up in a different location. If you head south, you are going to end up south inevitably.

Only by getting the situation out into the light will you begin to see what you are wrestling with. After naming it—rape, incest, sexual trafficking, poor choices, or whatever relevant title—you can then begin to diagnose a plan. Like the broken arm that will not heal on its own, you need to take your brokenness and call it for what it is before healing can begin.

And the emptiness can subside.

And your opinion of yourself can change.

And the hope for a better tomorrow can take form.

So take a deep breath and take some time to delve into your memories. What can you uncover? If you still need to do so, take every ounce of your strength and call your situation for what it is.

Go ahead.

It's your call.

And once you begin calling it, you'll start seeing it differently.

2

SEEING IT

A young man was walking through a supermarket to pick up a few things when he noticed an old lady following him around. Thinking nothing of it, he ignored her and continued on. Finally he went to the checkout line, but she got in front of him.

"Pardon me," she said, "I'm sorry if my staring at you has made you feel uncomfortable. It's just that you look just like my son, who just died recently."

"I'm very sorry," replied the young man, "is there anything I can do for you?"

"Yes," she said, "As I'm leaving, can you say 'Good bye, Mother!'?

It would make me feel so much better."

"Sure," answered the young man.

As the old woman was leaving, he called out, "Goodbye, Mother!"

As he stepped up to the checkout counter, he saw that his total was $127.50.

"How can that be?" he asked, "I only purchased a few things!"

"Your mother said that you would pay for her," said the clerk.[2]

Sometimes the truth reveals itself through utter transparency. The grass flaunts its green shade, or maybe brown if it's—ahem—my yard. On a sunny day, the sky dazzles us with its brilliant blue backdrop.

I can identify the uniform of an Army soldier, research a licensed architect, or reference details in a world history book. Driving down a town street, I can easily spot the stores offering sales by the beckoning, bold banners they display.

What makes the truth in these various conditions so apparent? These situations concern facts that can be touched, seen, or confirmed. Their circumstances allow for easy confirmation of the truth. However, the truth becomes hazier when it falls beyond the bounds of the touchable, seeable, or confirmable.

"I promise I told you everything."

"I have never known a nicer person than you."

"I always tell the truth."

"My boss doesn't even comprehend fairness."

"She never lies."

"I love you."

"I heard him say...."

Hmm, not so easy to detect the truthfulness anymore, is it? Because none of the above claims allow for clear-cut verification. Without question, truth still exists. But layers of unexposed thoughts and feelings may hide the truth by concealing selfish intentions and unrevealed facts. Then again, sometimes proposed truths don't even qualify as truths in the slightest degree but are only masquerades for straight-up, bold-faced lies.

A pastor, who holds dual master's degrees in therapy and counseling, once told me that what we feel follows what we believe. What we believe to be true, what we hold as the truth, directly affects and causes our feelings in response. To appreciate how our beliefs lead to our feelings, kick around some actual scenarios.

Example 1:

You look around your yard but do not see your dog. You believe your dog has wandered away again. Last time, you found him perched on the edge of a bustling four-lane road. In a split second, fear bubbles and heralds an urgency to search for him.

Example 2:

While entering an intersection, a cross-traffic vehicle runs the stop sign and decimates the rear end of your vehicle. Upon examining the damage, you see a steady stream of liquid puddling underneath your vehicle. You believe the liquid is potentially flammable, so you distance yourself from the scene and call for help.

As you may have noticed, both instances involve the touchable and confirmable. Once you find your dog, you feel relieved. You no longer feel threatened when the fire department arrives and confirms no fire danger.

So a progression emerges. Any time our beliefs receive validation, our feelings receive validation as a consequence.

THE PATTERN OF BELIEF

But what happens when we cannot confirm our beliefs through tangibility—when the truth is found only in others' words or processed in our hearts and minds? Without the allowance of time or affirmation, we take a stab at crafting a truth. Sometimes, *despite* sufficient time or affirmation, we still try to craft a more desirable or believable truth. We convince ourselves our version of the truth *is* accurate—*especially when the alternatives are too much to bear.* We try to justify and control the reasoning substantiating our preferred inclination. And we do not stop there. Then we take these manipulated truths and allow them to dictate how we feel and act.

He says he loves me and wants me to spend the night. He must *love me because no one has ever said that to me before. So how could I tell him no?*

She is so popular and knows all the latest gossip. Based on her intel, everyone finds the new girl at work annoying. Note to self: Avoid the new girl.

He insists he will repay me next week. Even though he has told me this for the last three weeks, I would not want to hurt his feelings or seem rude. I'm sure he means it this time so I will continue to wait for repayment.

My whole life, my parents have told me I am a failure. Parents are supposed to be the ones who know their children the best. If they don't believe in me, why would anyone else? So there's no use applying for that *job because they'd never want to hire someone like me.*

Do you see the pattern?

BELIEF ⟶ FEELING ⟶ ACTION

Our beliefs lead to our feelings which in turn dictate our actions.

Yet danger presents itself when we root our beliefs into anything less than the truth—when we let our beliefs be guided by the familiar rather than the factual.

And I will let you in on another danger: An enemy who understands all this is actively pursuing you.

Who is this enemy, you ask?

Well, although he has attacked everyone who has ever lived, he is gunning for a more noted target. That is, before he set his sights on us, he determined, first and foremost, to secure his position as God's enemy.

NO WRONG PLACE TO BEGIN

Just as we all have different life stories, we all come to the table with different experiences and opinions of God. I do not assume that every person possesses a positive view of God. In fact, the sensitive issues we are addressing could have distorted your view of God, and understandably so.

"How could there be a God and yet so much evil in the world?"

"If there was a God, why does He allow such bad things to happen?"

"If there was a God, where was He when I ..."

I hear you. And I believe that God hears you too. Please know you are asking weighty questions that are not only logical but also vital to ask. Perhaps your family shunned the thought of God. Maybe an acquaintance claimed to believe in God, but their version of God left nothing to desire of God. Would you say that you believed in God once but lost your belief when hurt shattered your life? Or maybe you never had exposure to or contemplated the idea of God. Countless possibilities exist for where you find yourself today, but none correspond to a "wrong" place from which to begin. God actually welcomes your questions, and He welcomes you—undeterred by your past or present stance. He knows we all come from a fallen world and does not hold that against us. He also knows that His and our enemy has been working for thousands of years to twist and taint peoples' views of Him.

So, yes, again—who is this enemy?

If you have access to a Bible or are open to hearing about it, you can find this enemy in the very first pages of the Bible. In the very first book of the Bible—Genesis.

Composed of sixty-six books, I like to think of the Bible as a collection of various personal stories that together form one giant, overarching narrative of all humanity. Unless you compare two identical Bibles, it's uncommon for two separate Bibles to display the same passages on the same pages because of variables such as publishers, print sizes, additional study materials, and translations. Hundreds and thousands of years ago, a translation referred to someone translating the Bible into a different language—from Hebrew to Greek, for instance. Today, however, Bible translations concern unique ways of expressing the same thought, as evidenced below.

> "Because of the Lord's great love we are not consumed, for His compassions never fail."
>
> Lamentations 3:22, NIV

> "God's loyal love couldn't have run out, His merciful love couldn't have dried up."
>
> Lamentations 3:22, MSG

> "The faithful love of the Lord never ends! His mercies never cease."
>
> Lamentations 3:22, NLT

Each verse expresses the same idea but through varied wording. Just as you might speak using words or expressions that differ from someone fifty years older than you, writers tailored Bible versions to individual audiences over numerous periods. No translation is better than another. Translations merely boil down to a matter of personal preference as you contemplate which is easiest to relate to or understand. And often, a particular translation will stir you depending on the verse or the season of your life.

SEEING AN ENEMY

But, regardless of the specific translation, if you pick up any Christian Bible, that Bible will always begin with the book of Genesis. And as I already told you, you will not need to flip too far to find this enemy for whom we are searching. The first chapter in Genesis explains the creation of the world. The second chapter in Genesis talks about the creation of man in that world. And by the third chapter—boom—an enemy appears.

> Now the serpent was more *crafty* than any of the wild animals the Lord God had made. He said to the woman, "Did God really say, 'You must not eat from any tree in the garden'?"
>
> The woman said to the serpent, "We may eat fruit from the trees in the garden, but God did say, 'You must not eat fruit from the tree that is in the middle of the garden, and you must not touch it, or you will die.'"
>
> "You will not certainly die," the serpent said to the woman.
>
> Genesis 3:1- 4, emphasis mine

Considering that we are reading only the third chapter of the Bible's first book, you might ask, "What is this serpent?" I mean, who likes a talking snake? Am I right? And why is this woman trying to carry on a conversation with it rather than trying to whack it with a tree limb? There you go with those good questions again!

The story introduces the woman as Eve, who God created to be a companion to the first man, Adam. Together, Adam and Eve live in the perfect world created in chapter 1 of Genesis. So the abrupt appearance of this serpent in chapter 3 spoils the scene. And while readers may approach this story through a lens of sincerity, the serpent is described as crafty. Bearing in mind that *crafty* is defined as "adept in the use of subtlety and cunning"³ and *cunning* means "characterized by wiliness and trickery,"⁴ though this snake's appearance seems to come out of nowhere, his description should alert us to the fact that his appearance on the scene may be anything *but* unplanned. In actuality, this serpent will further be portrayed in this passage and throughout the rest of the Bible as an enemy—to Adam and Eve, to us, but above all, to God Himself.

Whether you are taking in this story for the first time or the hundredth time, I want to point out a helpful tip. The very first recorded words of the serpent—what are they? *"Did God really say…"*

After Eve's response to his question, what are the second recorded words of the serpent? *"You will not certainly die."*

Friends, we are not dealing with a regular snake on any given level. This conversation does not spontaneously transpire between an innocent woman and an innocent snake. This snake intended to interject doubt between the woman and God. To do so, it tossed out a conscious contradiction of God's original words to propose that God had limited Adam and Eve from eating fruit from *any* tree in the garden. Then, it piqued suspicion in Eve's mind about the trustworthiness of God's intent by twisting the fundamental truth of God's words. Essentially, the snake's sales pitch asserted, "You will not die as God said. God is a liar." Yet the only thing its sales tactics could guarantee was distortion: *God* wasn't the liar. The smooth-talking snake itself was!

So I want you to hold on to this thought: When this serpent— this evil enemy—first spoke, he chose distortion and lies. His primary objective depended upon undermining, contradicting, confusing, distorting, or twisting God's truths—in any way he could.

While thousands of years have passed since this baited exchange, the enemy still lurks. *And his prime method of attack remains unchanged: His go-to play still relies on lies.*

But did you notice that the serpent didn't blow his cover with blatant deceit? He did not attempt to claim "God is not God" or "God said to eat rocks rather than fruit from the trees." Eve would have walked away within seconds if he had exposed his intents like that. No, his systematic planning shrouded a more crafty and cunning agenda than that.

SEEING OUR MOTIVATIONS

The English writer Samuel Johnson advises, "Actions are visible, though motives are secret."[5] In all reality, we can never get to the bottom of someone else's motives—all the reasons why they do what they do. But we had best know our own motives to stay on the safe path of truth.

What do I mean?

Most motives arise from the desire for a goal that, in and of itself, does not equate with any evil aspiration.

Some people long to be loved.

Some desire success.

Some seek acceptance.

Some want to provide well for their family.

Some seek lots of friends.

None of these desires equate to an evil thing. Loving, being loved, appreciating family and friendship, attaining enjoyable and productive careers—God included all these things in His original plans, framed in the first two chapters of Genesis. Adam and Eve loved each other and basked in God's love as well. They experienced friendship with each other and with God every day as they walked and talked together. Their labors were not frustrated, and they tasted joy and fulfillment as fruits of their work.

But. But then the crafty, cunning world of a sinful nature crept in. Even today, sinful nature does not enter and boldly proclaim its intent. No, it still sneaks in without a sound.

23

SEEING IT

Carefully. Slowly. Until it burrows so deep under your skin that you cannot even remember being free from its commanding control.

Reagan has decided that this is her year to get healthy. Great! Gym membership and cute workout clothes? Check. Grocery stops look different now—more fruit, less fruity flavored candies. Ready to battle a few pesky pounds, she has a game plan. She has researched all the top influencers' blogs. Studied their habits and routines—and their photos of proof. Gripped by determination, she logs more hours at the gym and digs in for two more reps here, ten more minutes there. But the weight remains. No change. Frustration leads Reagan to wonder whether skipping a meal would make a difference.

To her pleasant surprise, the weight finally begins to disappear. *Gravy—no! New expression: Strawberry!* So why not try eating less for each remaining meal? Even lower numbers appear on the scale! At long last, the person staring back at her in the mirror has changed. Her friends claim she is more irritable these days, but she still has that one area there and that one place here that does not resemble the online photos she longs to replicate. However, most days now, exhaustion overtakes her, leaving her unable to muster the energy for more reps or exercise time. Her last option? Well, purging, of course. Not forever. Just until she can shed a couple more pounds.

Wow! How did she get there?

Chloe wants a successful career. Wonderful! So she worked throughout high school and earned a sizeable college scholarship. While others partied, she studied. Her hard work paid off, and Chloe got her dream job straight out of college. The hours exceed the typical full-time job, but she enjoys it. Her colleagues often like to unwind together at the bar after a long day. While Chloe has never been one for drinking, she figures a refusal to go would not help her status. So she goes—a lot. Glass after glass, she hears stories and rumors and picks up on affairs the others have when they travel for work. She sees the material things success has provided for them: enhanced bodies, expensive labels, and exotic vacations. Their lives sound adventurous. Spontaneous. Glamorous.

And now Chloe can follow suit, for her colleagues have let her in their circle—so much so, they have also let Chloe in on their next major plan. It requires a slight dishonesty in the figures on the company ledgers. Not that the company would ever miss it. Why, such a minor amount is not different from a perk or a small bonus. But if Chloe passes on the chance, would the others fear she might expose them? If so, they would probably pull strings to get her fired. Participation, just this once, should be enough to protect her job and appease her colleagues.

Yikes! How again?

Few people would categorize themselves, or Reagan and Chloe, as evil people with evil motives. But motives pose risks: They can mushroom and easily eclipse our desire for truth. Before we know it, we find ourselves willing to do things we would never have entertained. Say things we never would have previously said. Step after step, we can plunge deep into a world we never planned on entering. Not giant leap by giant leap. Rather, little step by little step is all it takes to lead to an eventual blinding.

So bringing the conversation back to here and now, where do you find yourself today? What motivations drive you? What is your number one goal, desire, dream, or wish? If you are unsure, ask yourself: "If I could have anything, it would be (fill in the blank)."

As for myself, my greatest desire when I was a young girl was to feel loved. More than anything, I wanted a relationship that provided me with recognition and a chance to love and be loved. My reasonable desire arose from the part of our human nature hardwired to crave love.

Therefore, my initial motivation could not be criticized or condemned as evil. But my innocence was contaminated when life happened. Life—with its ups and downs, and sometimes more downs. Life—with its sinful and hurtful experiences. Life—with its continual bombardment of truth-twisting lies.

Most often, loneliness, hurt, and desperation were the only companions I entertained. My desire to feel love became my tunnel vision. I was willing to say and believe whatever anyone asked of me as long as I could gain their approval and acceptance. I accepted others' opinions and ideas over my own because I regarded my life as less valuable or less worthy when compared to their lives. My naïve assessments allowed the world to dictate the truth to me.

TRUTH CONCOCTIONS

As I shared earlier, I wish I could tell you that I turned my life around after the person I loved and thought loved me admitted to using me. But I did not. By then, his betrayal represented just another hurt piled onto an already growing mountain of pain. No, the raw truth was too painful of an alternative: I had been taken advantage of, and the person whom I had deemed most trustworthy had been the one to violate my trust. Yet the harshest devastation was that the person who I presumed would fulfill my deepest dream had, instead, brought about my greatest nightmare. So I subconsciously created my own "truth" to combat the painful facts of reality and tried my best to bury, deny, and run from the hard truth. Far from turning my mess around, all I did was look the other way.

And as my truths got blurred and downright screwed up, my actions followed south in the attempt to attain my desire. Without the guiding anchor of truth, my life sailed far off course. I bought the lie that I was unlovable. I fell for the lie that I had to sacrifice everything for the chance of a relationship with others. And I swallowed the lie that I had destroyed any possibility of being considered good. I believed it all—hook, line, and sinker.

Amid my hurt, I surmised two things: (1) Something is wrong with me. Very. Very. Wrong. I do not have what it takes to merit a loving relationship. (2) I am ruined now after having sex. I have missed reaching the ultimate bar of goodness. Purity is a one-way street. Nothing can be undone or taken back, so why even pretend to be good anymore? I can never be anything other than what I am right now.

Those lies became my utmost life-guiding beliefs—truth concoctions I mixed up with equal parts of pain, confusion, and bitterness. As could be expected, recipes are only as good as their ingredients, and when you mix up such toxic ingredients, prepare for a dose of life poisoning!

What truth recipes have you mixed up in the laboratory of your heart? If you had choices, what truths did you believe that led you to your actions? If you had no choice, have you formed faulty truths based on those hurts?

And how are these "truths" blurring your present and future choices?

I wish I could tell you the specific lies the enemy has snuck into your life. I also wish we could find our remedies in quick, easy, and similar diagnoses. But the enemy's lies mutate—taking on whatever form or variation required to wreak the most damage possible for each individual. So, unfortunately, my initial motivation to be loved may not match your initial motivation, and the points at which I fell for the lies will not necessarily predict your stumbling blocks.

It may take considerable time to dig to the basis of our truths—the roots of our thoughts and feelings. Roots that are so familiar and planted so deep within our core, we do not even notice them because we have grown accustomed to them as just a normal part of our life's terrain. Exposing the basis of our beliefs presents a hard step, but we all need this necessary step to find what drives our feelings and actions before we can take a further step toward healing.

Remember, we cannot determine what drives others. Even when their actions seem easy to read, our job does not entail figuring out others' motives. (Trust me, you could never undertake a more hopeless, unending task than trying to read others. Ask me how I know!) *Your path to healing will not require you to justify or even understand another person's actions.* You could never plumb the depth of another person's soul. Our own fathomless soul is enough to require all our attention.

DUMPING LOADS OF LIES

We have no choice but to dig down to the bottom of the hurt, pains, and injustices to uncover what beliefs we are now building our life and actions upon. For some, that means sifting through layers. For others like me, it means digging up some massive brick walls. For some, that means going back over several months or years. For others, it means going back. Way back.

Do you remember the story that opened this chapter—the unsuspecting man who fell prey to a con woman who exploited his honest, trusting nature at the grocery store? I would venture to say that, whatever your story, every one of our stories has an element of exploitation or hurt somewhere along the lines. Lucky guess? Not really. Remember Genesis chapter 3? That story began a grievous unraveling that has only continued in human lives for thousands of years. It's a sad fact, but the enemy's lies have succeeded in burning you, me, and every other human who has ever lived.

So if you have grown sick of your hurt and belief patterns, then it is time to dump the grocery cart your enemy has loaded with lies.

Now we can see the enemy for what he is worth—nothing.

We can recognize where the enemy's lies have gotten us—in the pits.

So now, let's start to see how he got us there—so we can get out!

Start to see what lies he has shoved into the nooks of our hearts.

See what has sprouted from the seeds of those lies.

See what we have chosen to believe versus what we have neglected to believe.

I think that the Bible prevails as the only gauge of truth in this messed-up world. To me, the Bible's grand story, spanning thousands of years and lives, epitomizes the most extraordinary account of love and redemption ever written. A story written to the lost and the broken of the world to convince you there is more to the world's story than you could ever know!

Since I consider the Bible our only source of truth, then I find it logical for the Bible to mark the starting line for uncovering where our thoughts have gone off track. I pray that each of you has a trusted individual to turn to and access to a printed or an online Bible. But even if you lack these things, I want to reassure you that I, too, felt completely and utterly alone on my journey. While I did have access to a Bible, I made the foolish choice not to utilize it for plenty of years, and in doing so, I unknowingly prolonged the duration of my journey.

Regardless of what you have at your disposal, I want to relieve any doubt: *You have all that you need.* Yes, God speaks through the Bible, but He also communicates with us in a million other ways. And yes, wise mentors or godly friends can produce huge dividends in our lives. But God's wisdom? Unmatched. God's comfort? Beyond compare. So no matter how we feel, we are never truly alone. At least not in the spiritual sense. There is a spiritual world—a spiritual war—engaged all around us, and the Bible bolsters us with the remarkable promise that God will never leave us. Ever. He sees every tear. Hears every prayer. Holds us as we cry ourselves to sleep. And He longs to mend all our hurt and pain.

And if we could see Him as He draws near to wipe the tears rolling down our faces, we would know that He operates not with an air of superiority or judgment but with scarred hands. Scarred from the same pain, hurt, and evil you face today, too. He knows. He knows it all—every story, *your* story. From the beginning to the end: God knows.

So if you cannot decipher the truth yet, I believe you will if you keep seeking. Sometimes this requires a prayer to simply ask, "God, please show me where hurt, lies, or misconceptions linger." And then wait. God might speak suddenly. Other times, His answer will come later. Just keep your heart's eyes and ears open. You never know how God may talk to you because He caters to the various ways we hear best. Some hear Him while hiking in the forest. Me? If I were in the woods, I would be distracted by the mosquitoes eating me alive. But I appreciate creative outlets, so I might find hearing from Him easier while beholding His latest painted sunset.

He also speaks when you least expect Him—in the less-than-big moments. While folding laundry. Writing that paper. Or serving the next customer.

And He can speak anywhere: in a dorm room, a jail cell, or a work cubicle.

Have patience. This process does take time. But do not go easy on yourself either—you are in a war for your life.

We cannot exchange the truth for a lie and come out unscathed. Eve did not. We will not.

But we will survive when we battle armed with the protection of truth.

"You will seek me and find me when you seek me with all your heart" (Jeremiah 29:13).

Truth has been there all along, but it has been covered by confusion and buried underneath pain for so long that it might feel like you're seeing it for the first time.

So leave no stone unturned.

Because the truth is worthy of any effort required to find it.

Can you see it yet?

PART 2

THE PLOT THICKENS

3

FLIPPING IT

"My parents realized I needed to get my eyes checked when 7 yr [sic] old me saw some round hay bales in a field and asked if those were the buffaloes we were going to see."

If you find yourself laughing, you probably have good eyesight! Or perhaps you laugh because you can relate to this story due to your poor eyesight! Either way, impaired vision can drastically shift our perceptions and experiences. Legendary stories abound of people who never knew that trees stretched beyond their trunks or that roofs crowned houses. These unfortunate people lived with a distorted version of normal—all because of their impaired eyesight. They had no idea what they were missing.

So far, I am blessed to have inherited good eyesight. But for full disclosure, I am referring to my *physical* eyesight. My emotional sight often fails to achieve a 20/20 vision. As I have already shared, emotional turmoil overshadowed my life for years. And if you buy that, I have conned you with what qualifies as my version of a leafless tree! Because the truth is, my internal life remained a mess for decades.

Our stories and our memories all shape us. The ones that feel like yesterday. The images we have replayed over and over in our minds. We must know every square inch of them. Undoubtedly, we can recall with vivid detail every heart-numbing, soul-crushing moment. I can guarantee that you do. And to a fair extent, we can claim to know our stories.

But as the poor buffalo-chasing boy demonstrated, he, too, felt that he could accurately perceive his experiences and surroundings. This discrepancy leaves us to face that our eyesight can mislead us. Our vision can fool us. Our memories and beliefs can all lead to emotions that function off-kilter in some senses.

Please hear me—I am *not* suggesting what happened to you did not happen. I am *not* asking you to deny any reality. Clearly, you get the big picture! That seven-year-old boy may not have known he was looking at a hay bale, but he knew it was something big!

No, I am only proposing that you genuinely try to reexamine the circumstances. To uncover any pieces you might have previously missed or accidentally overlooked. For example, it took me a while to perceive that I was not the center of a particular guy's world as I had hoped. And it took me years to realize that I had said, "No."

WHERE YOU ARE VERSUS WHERE YOU WANT TO BE

But how can you see what you have never seen before? You pull together every weapon at your disposal: When you combine calling it—naming your experience for what it is—with seeing it—with truth rather than with your preferences—you will create a reaction that produces a switch in your beliefs and feelings about your situation.

Once I realized the truth that I had made sufficient efforts to stop his attempts, I could call my encounter date rape. Then, after working to process and further accept what date rape meant, I underwent a switch. My impressions did an about-face. I approached the memories as a new person. The switch allowed me to see the whole situation and, more importantly, the other person through a completely different lens using completely different eyesight.

When assessing your weapons, truth serves a dual purpose. Truth will not only supply a brand-new perspective on your situation, but the truth will also function as an excellent microscope to decipher your motives. For it can magnify and reveal the internal reasons that led to your external actions. So armed with whatever truths you have gained so far, can you narrow down which desire—while not necessarily wrong or evil—may have influenced your choices? Delving deeper, where have you applied your desires or beliefs to innocent bystanders? Or if your situation arose from someone else's desires rather than your own, where have your beliefs led you regarding that time, that person, and yourself? Have you begun stereotyping or judging others based on your fears or assumptions?

Digging this far below the surface, I suspect you will find that, in struggling to achieve your intent, you have drifted remarkably far from where your desires first started. Though it stings to realize the contrast, this recognition exposes the currents hindering your ability to live more fully and wisely.

I will go out on a sturdy limb here and say the chances are high that you are dealing with an unhealthy relationship or situation if this book even remotely resonates with you. If you are sexually involved with someone outside of marriage— even if it has been your choice—you are standing on shaky grounds, at best. If you are in a situation in which you do not have choices, such as continued incest or sex trafficking, you are navigating minefields.

Yet, fully appreciating the vast gulf between where you are and where you want to be provides the momentum to press on toward a place of health and healing. Whichever avenue you need to take, any route toward healing will always head in the opposite direction of an abuser or manipulator. Abusers and manipulators only use you for personal fulfillment, and neither leads you to a place of safety or love.

Sincere love reverses the self-centered norm and puts others first. The old saying "true love waits" needs to be revived because true love *will* wait, even though waiting is difficult. But restraining impulse and choosing to wait proves a desire for *you*—rather than what you can *do* or *give*. And when love is patient, it exemplifies its strength to stay not only early in the relationship but also later when hard times or temptations arise. For sincere love operates by the guidance of long-term dependability.

RETHINKING SEX

I never would have included the terms "unselfish" or "staying power" in my earliest descriptions of sex. Perhaps you remember my childhood definition was "something gross and repulsive?" Despite my later maturing, my definition only grew to "what I must do to have a boy like me." Both negative views were formulated from unhealthy situations, mind you, but I made matters worse by acting upon their harmful guidance.

Just as I had to redefine my life through the lens of truth, I needed to examine the principles of sex before I could confirm that I was operating with unobstructed vision. Vision that could spot the differences between right and wrong, a trunk and a tree, or a bale of hay and a buffalo.

Turning to the Bible, I found evidence of an act created to be the exact opposite of what I had experienced—as a child or as a young adult. When discussing marriage or sex, it is common for the Bible to reference the principle, "That is why a man leaves his father and mother and is united to his wife, and they become one flesh" (Genesis 2:24). Jesus Himself even quoted these words when disputing those of His time who supported the prevalent practice of unmerited divorce.

> "Haven't you read," he replied, "that at the beginning the Creator 'made them male and female,' and said, 'For this reason a man will leave his father and mother

and be united to his wife, and the two will become one flesh'? *So they are no longer two, but one flesh.* Therefore what God has joined together, let no one separate."

Matthew 19:4-6, emphasis mine

The Bible sets out a couple of distinct and notable precedents for sex. First, sex separates the marital relationship from all other roles. Second, sex blends what were two identities into one.

To further drive home the unique, reverent nature of sex, Jesus continued His conversation by adding an important detail, "I want to tell you that anyone who divorces his wife, *except for sexual immorality*, and marries another woman commits adultery" (Matthew 19:9, emphasis mine). While not condoning casual divorce, Jesus clarified that sexual immorality does provide a solid justification for divorce.

And though the Bible does not explicitly state the accommodation, it is my heartfelt belief that it would allow for divorce on the grounds of abuse as well, for Jesus did command husbands to love their wives as Christ loved the church. And how did Jesus love the church? He died for it! He paid our penalty so we would not have to suffer or die. If He went to such lengths to *remove* our suffering, He would never condone the *infliction* of suffering—especially within marriage, an institution meant to provide safety.

To assure you that the Bible does not present divorce as a flippant nor celebrated step, I should highlight Malachi 2:16, which reads, "The man who hates and divorces his wife," says the Lord, the God of Israel, "does violence to the one he should protect." So if God equates divorce with an act of violence, why did Jesus specify sexual immorality as an *allowance* for divorce?

Wrestling with this question requires us first to ponder sexual immorality. Sexual immorality occurs when either spouse fails to uphold their end of the covenantal relationship concerning sexual relations. Sexual immorality manifests itself in various ways: a physical affair, a pornography addiction, or the use of technology to obtain sexual gratification, to name a few. Any of the previous actions break the pledge of trust within a marriage and result in broken bonds and shattered lives. These ramifications lead me to wonder, did Jesus provide sexual immorality as a legitimate reason for divorce because He knew that the damage of sexual sin could surpass even the damage of divorce?

Indeed, sex, as God designed it, served to unite two individuals. One plus one does equal two, but additional mathematics apply when evaluating the topic of sex within marriage. While multiplication factors into childbearing, it cannot appear in a formula for marital intimacy. Marital intimacy's best chance for survival is if addition and subtraction do not enter the equation—the addition of other individuals or the subtraction of either spouse. Yet the most imperative mathematical marriage fact insists that no division should occur within the marriage: The two individuals are to remain undivided, united for life.

NO GUARDRAILS

I can only speak for myself, but my sexual experiences did not incorporate any form of unity. Instead, they added misery and pain to my daily life and subtracted several facets from my life—my joy, peace, and self-esteem. And they interjected division as well—in my ideals and relationships. So I began to see why God prescribed abstinence as the preferred path until one could experience sex within the context of marriage: He preferred to replace a no strings attached mindset with a commitment to provide both physical and emotional safety. For life. When done right, marriage mimics the forever relationship God wants to have with each of us. A relationship that stays in the boat regardless of the wait, regardless of the storm, and regardless of the cost. From this perspective, premarital sex wars against every aspect of God's design. Premarital sex is a contradiction—an oxymoron like jumbo shrimp. It robs the notion of forever and substitutes it with a one-night stand, a quick thrill, or a greedy game. Sex requires the safe confines and limitations of marriage as guardrails, much like bumper guards in bowling. If you remove the bumper guards from sex, you get premarital sex and gutters.

Many people would disagree because they perceive confines and limitations as shackles. But think about driving a vehicle. Driving can permit significant freedom to go places and enjoy activities that would otherwise be impossible. But what if, one day, the rules of the road expired? No more traffic lights to obey. No stop signs to notice. No particular side of the road to drive on. Speed limit—what's that? Driver's license—who needs that? Everyone gains permission to get where they need to—in whatever manner they choose. Can you imagine the chaos? I can picture cars weaving in and out of each other, heading in every direction. Adrenaline is pumping all over town as people experiment to find just how fast they can get from Point A to Point B. Kids, no longer bound by an age limit, jump to get their chance behind the wheel! Road rage erupts all over town as each driver claims his right to be the first through an intersection. Bedlam, alone, reigns.

So it's evident that you can't call me an adrenaline junkie, as the mere idea of these potential disasters has me considerably unnerved! Yet, it does not seem fanatical or unrealistic to believe that we owe some gratitude for the limitations placed on driving. The restrictions make it possible to drive—and arrive—safely. Why, then, view the Biblical limitations placed on sex as anything other than beneficial? Because, like the traffic laws, the Biblical guardrails surrounding sex ensure safe navigation in life—without incurring detours, blockades, or injury.

My experiences? No guardrails.

No *wonder* I was where I was.

No *wonder* I felt how I felt.

No *wonder* I thought I hated sex.

No *wonder* I was left feeling unfulfilled.

No *wonder* sex didn't equate to love.

Huh. Sex and love were actually two different things.

So after finding the Biblical perspective, no other choice existed but to flip my definition of sex.

For my previous definition, lay toppled in pieces.

But I pieced together that I could no longer look at sex the same.

FLIPPING WHAT DOESN'T WORK

With many new realizations to explore, my mind spun from the ramifications. For the first time, I was absorbing what God intended sex to be. Scores of misperceptions had left me in shambles. Like the lawless driving scenario, my reckless living ended with reckless results. But I could finally identify the senseless, poor choices that led me to this mess.

Sometimes, our mistakes take us by surprise. Other times, our bad choices are unmistakable. But to some extent, we all live and learn as we go. So you cannot blame yourself for not having everything figured out—no one does. Thomas Edison once said, "I have not failed. I've just found 10,000 ways that won't work."[6] With good reason, Edison took risks in science and life to find solutions to his questions. If Edison had succumbed to the disappointment or embarrassment of his setbacks or miscalculations, he never would have found answers or celebrated later success.

Yet inventions, even ones as wonderful as Edison's light bulb, can't begin to compare to you! Beyond question, your body encompasses far more significance than any technological advancement—bar none! And despite Edison's necessary risk-taking, I am not advocating taking risks with your body. My point is only to illustrate that not every mistake is born from an unmistakably poor choice. As Edison knew, our mistakes are often our best teachers in disguise. In actuality, our greatest threat is usually not the mistake itself but failing to *learn* from the mistake.

So if you were ever in a situation you were not adequately equipped to handle, I am sorry. If you had no guidance to steer yourself to safety and were taken advantage of, I feel your pain. You no longer need to blame yourself for a part you weren't willing to play.

However, in situations where you did make regrettable choices, though you will need to own those choices, those choices will no longer own *you*. You will use your previous poor choices not to define you but to train you—into a wiser you.

I pray you haven't racked up a tally anywhere close to 10,000 mistakes. Especially regarding situations involving sex, I long for the day when no girl or woman needs to count beyond zero! But the fact that I am writing this book, and you are reading it, proves such a day has not yet arrived and convinces me that more women still need their definitions of sex flipped.

Seeing sex as envisioned in the Bible, rather than as it appeared in my life, spotlighted some simple explanations for why all my strivings fell flat. When my strongest desire was to be loved, I became motivated to do all I could to get love, which included sacrificing my values, my body, and my heart piece after piece. I possessed a natural desire but not enough truth to obtain that desire. So I had grasped, stretched, and leaped in my attempts to attain love.

But once I perceived the truth that sex did not equate to love and that sex was not the only vehicle to attain love, I knew I needed to ditch some things. Please understand I did not lose my original desire. I did not lose my innate craving for love and companionship. But what I lost was my willingness to continue down the unsuccessful paths I had repeatedly taken in search of love. Counting my mistakes, I had to admit. I had found quite a few ways that would not work.

If I wanted a committed, mutual love, I could no longer give myself away with abandon. I needed to search for someone who would respect me enough not to ask me to live outside God's boundaries. And if it took time to identify a person who operated that way, I needed to wait and not settle for less than God's best in my life.

I still had a desire. But now, my actions that stemmed from that motivating desire could be grounded in truth rather than reckless wants.

In your own life, do you see lies blurring the evidence of truth?

Hoping to forget or deny, are you attempting to block, bury, or ignore painful past or present circumstances?

How is the pain changing or controlling you?

Has your capability to love or trust diminished or disappeared?

Are you able to identify emotional walls you have constructed for protection?

Can you accurately assess what you want most?

If so, can you articulate your measures or lengths to fulfill that desire?

Do you detect motivation that may have crossed the line to become greed or disregard?

Where have your actions led you?

Like me, can you concede that you have landed far from your original desire?

Despite my intense hunger to be loved, I found myself alone. Despite yearning for connection and intimacy, my best attempts only left me feeling abandoned, used, and exposed. But my ways did not line up with God's ways. As much as I may have prayed to God for help, I could not receive His complete rescue until I was willing to take hold of a new way. By taking hold of His hand. By looking to Him for the things I could not get from this world.

Such as unconditional love.

Secure and unshakeable intimacy.

Solid, trustworthy promises.

Safety.

And my definition of sex.

HIRING A PROFESSIONAL OVER AN AMATEUR

Make no mistake. God is never further than your side. And I believe His Word when it tells us He sees every tear that falls. (An impressive feat to consider if you, too, suspect you've shed enough tears to fill an ocean!) Without fail, His caring ear never misses a single prayer you pray, and He longs to have a relationship with you more than you can imagine.

But God sets the standard for the Ultimate Gentleman. He will not push or force His way into your life. He will not harshly bend or break you into submission. Instead, with inexhaustible patience, He will wait for you until you are ready for the next step. Until you are willing to drop your weary soul into His strong arms of rest, collapse your beaten-down self into His lap, curl up in surrender, and allow Him to carry you.

Only with our allowance will He work with us to move us from where we are—to where He wants us to be.

Only when we stop. Stop striving. Stop fighting. Stop running. Stop burying. Stop breaking. Stop continuing to do life on our terms and our limited vision.

My emotional eyesight finally adjusted to take in my surroundings properly: My ways were not working. So I concluded, if my methods weren't working, what would it hurt to try God's ways?

I had defined sex as gross or some box I had to check off as a means to an end.

But God had defined it differently.

It wasn't a means to get to something better. Nor was there a risk of losing oneself in a game if an exclusive relationship was the game plan.

The definition hinged on intent: Would sex serve unselfish or selfish aspirations? Because selfishness, on your part or another's, will sell out your best long-term interest for a temporary gain every single time. And that *will* leave a lingering, gross impression—or a lingering, gross definition. But according to God's description, when unselfishness and commitment drive the plan, sex is good.

God views sex this way because He is the Creator, CEO, and designer of sex. He holds the blueprints.

Any building attempt will stand its best chance when it follows blueprints—not gut instincts, feelings, trial and error, or relying on previous experience. Series about real estate buying or selling, do-it-yourself home projects, and home remodeling saturate cable television. Reality television series have shed new light on the word "flip." To tell the truth, I can't even utter the word without imagining one of the previous television examples. If you are unfamiliar with the idea, flipping a house means buying a home in desperate need of structural or cosmetic renovation and performing the necessary work to sell the house at a profit.

The lure of these shows relies on the inevitable setbacks that always arise. Either the show starts with a dilapidated house that looks like it would crumble if you blew on it hard enough, or the construction team unearths some unseen variable once they strip away the cosmetic layers. Leaking pipes. Termite damage. Unstable foundation. Sadly, however, these hazards can pop up anywhere and are not limited to housing renovations. Appreciate the accurate comparisons between these terms and my earliest definitions of sex. My definition was also shaky, leaking at the seams, and rotted away from years of infestation. While these disasters might work well for television ratings, they do not bode well for life foundations.

Beyond the disastrous surprises, the real comedy in these home improvement shows erupts when untrained people try to tackle or remedy the daunting problems themselves. Sometimes the situation deteriorates from bad to worse in the blink of an eye! This wise observation from the famed oil well firefighter, Red Adair, would halt these shows in their tracks: "If you think it's expensive to hire a professional to do the job, wait until you hire an amateur."[7]

I only qualified as an amateur attempting to perform a professional's job.

I tried to draft my own blueprints.

But the scales did not work—they lacked accuracy.

I had unearthed a hazardous environment requiring remediation.

Leaks, cracks, and debris from my weathered life exposed the conspicuous need for inspection.

Their existence pointed to the inadequacy of my efforts and ingenuity in building my life.

My amateur methods prompted further damage.

How do you stand today? Solid or shaking? Secure or patched?

For me, standing in the rubble of my ruins, the scales tipped.

I had finally had enough.

I put down my hammer.

I couldn't fix my brokenness.

I put down my paint bucket—the hurt kept bleeding through no matter how many times I tried to cover it.

I took my blueprints, the ones outlining my stance on sex, and crumpled them.

Then I headed straight to the Professional. To the Designer and Creator of all—our hearts, our lives, and sex.

Life had flipped me.

But I was ready to start flipping it back.

How about you?

4

CREATING IT

Good.

The Creation story in Genesis 1 and 2 repeats that word often. After examining a newly created piece of the universe, God always deemed it "good."

That poses an obvious question: How much good do you see when you look at the world around you? Oh, we might catch glimpses of good in the media. Sometimes the evening news highlights a local dog's rescue from neglect, or a blurb about a Hollywood celebrity's generosity to a sick child may cycle across the internet.

But, typically, the stories of injustice, oppression, war, and fighting—ones without a shred of good—far outweigh the hopeful accounts.

So how can the Creation story prove relevant today? Why pore over a story written several thousand years ago? Why taunt us with the fact that life was not always as we see it today? How could the Creation story possibly apply to any of us?

The answers might surprise you.

What if we look at the story one day at a time?

DAY ONE: LIGHT IS GOOD

And God said, "Let there be light," and there was light. God saw that the light was good, and He separated the light from the darkness. God called the light "day," and the darkness He called "night." And there was evening, and there was morning—the first day.

Genesis 1:3-5

The inception of Creation began by dealing with the darkness that enshrouded the universe. By speaking, "Let there be light," God deliberately separated the darkness. He could have ordered the Creation days in any manner of His choosing, but He chose to address the darkness first. Light burst onto the scene, and God deemed it a good thing.

Has the dark of night ever overcome you in an unknown area of town or while walking on a trail in the woods? Even if you've ever struggled to inch through a dark room and avoid stubbed toes, you can quickly identify light as a good thing! We appreciate the light of the Sun during the day, and we value artificial inventions such as streetlights, flashlights, and lamps to create light for us during the night. But do these examples represent the riveting reasons why Day One of the Creation story applies to us today?

Not in the slightest.

As it happens, the Bible also speaks beyond its literal message to address a symbolic level. In the same manner that a snake can represent an evil enemy, light and dark can represent more too.

Darkness. This word describes the universe's initial state in the Creation story, but it also describes how each of our stories begins. We are all born into an unfortunate and automatic darkness courtesy of sin. Although our sinful nature is involuntarily assigned, it is not randomly designated as evidence of a wrongful act that we or anyone in our genealogy ever committed—unless we are tracing our lineage all the way back to Adam and Eve! Yet, since Adam and Eve sinned, every human life has been destined to face an unavoidable struggle with sin, and as we are discovering, sin fights with a blinding force. It aims to distort and remove any truth from our life. But for the most part, sin seeks to alienate us from God's presence.

With incessant ambition, our enemy schemes to turn us from God because God remains the author and source of light. And His light, alone, holds the solution for sin's darkness. As He illuminates the shadows and corners where we hide, He pulls the curtain back on sin and exposes its fraudulent schemes. When we see that sin teeters on a flimsy framework of lies, it doesn't seem as enticing anymore, and the darkness loses its appeal. Stepping into the light, we find that things look different! And now our lives and choices will look different, too, because we no longer walk in darkness—we walk in light. No longer shackled to sin, we find freedom in the light. No more stumbling. No more hiding.

God hasn't lost His creative spirit. Bring Him your darkness, and watch what He creates: Light! Truth! And it's all good.

DAY TWO: Separating "What Is" From "What Was"

And God said, "Let there be a vault between the waters to separate water from water." So God made the vault and separated the water under the vault from the water above it. And it was so. God called the vault "sky." And there was evening, and there was morning—the second day.

Genesis 1:6-8

On Day Two, God continued distinguishing the world's former state from its future state. And now, with light to illuminate His creation, God's next project was to separate the waters.

I am sure we have all studied the atmosphere at some point, whether at an elementary level or a more scholarly pursuit. Yet we only need to check the daily weather forecast to understand that water exists in our atmosphere and causes the humidity and the rains that we feel. Likewise, water is present below the sky but in other forms, such as oceans, bays, rivers, or lakes.

Granted, I recognize that we are not waterways, but plunging into Day Two, God's approach should snag our attention. God calculated that one particular technique would best advance His creation: separation.

The light and darkness of Day One entailed a realm with which we were not yet familiar. While some people have traveled to space, their explorations were still limited. For instance, no living person has glimpsed other galaxies or stepped on another planet. So in comparison, Day Two brought the Creation story closer to our level through a more relatable, personal step. God was coming near, and He was shaking things up. God's creative kingdom had begun to pierce through, and "what is" would no longer resemble "what was."

Separation. This notion is also necessary today when we choose to live our lives with a revised approach. We can't keep operating as we did before if we resolve to leave the darkness and its lies. We possess light now, so we don't have to live as if the darkness still hinders us. Our best approach requires separating our past selves, patterns, beliefs, and actions from our new identities and behaviors.

God's creativity flowed through the days of Creation, and it has begun to flow through our story as well: Look out, "what was." You're about to get washed away.

DAY THREE: A GOOD LIFE SOURCE

And God said, "Let the water under the sky be gathered to one place, and let dry ground appear." And it was so. God called the dry ground "land," and the gathered waters He called "seas." And God saw that it was good. Then God said, "Let the land produce vegetation: seed-bearing plants and trees on the land that bear fruit and seed in it, according to their various kinds." And it was so. The land produced vegetation: plants bearing seed according to their kinds and trees bearing fruit with seed in it according to their kinds. And God saw that it was good. And there was evening, and there was morning—the third day.

Genesis 1:9-13

God is the ultimate gardener. Judging by Day Three, if God decrees it, fertile land and abundant vegetation will appear. He sprinkled plants, trees, fruit, and seeds across the earth like confetti. With your mind's eye, imagine lush, green trees overflowing with mouthwatering fruits and plants bursting with colorful, fragrant blooms. Now, envision that in all directions, and you have Day Three.

Sound like the place to be? *Umm, yes, please.* Well, Jesus said that we could definitely fit in this landscape—as a branch.

"I am the true vine, and My Father is the gardener. Remain in Me, as I also remain in you. No branch can bear fruit by itself; it must remain in the vine. Neither can you bear fruit unless you remain in Me. I am the vine; you are the branches. If you remain in Me and I in you, you will bear much fruit; apart from Me you can do nothing."

John 15:1, 4-5

While vines can sustain life, branches, on the other hand, depend on a life source. If a branch does not obtain the sustenance it needs, it cannot thrive, produce fruit, or even stay alive. This sustainment is not satisfied through a one-time connection but demands a constant connection. Yet, when a branch is suitably attached to a vine, spontaneous, lush growth occurs in the branch.

Similarly, if we affix ourselves to a true Vine, we, too, will unveil some lush vegetation of our own. Our lives will generate an appealing quality to others, *not* because of our circumstances but because of how we grow. God didn't deem the vegetation in the Creation story good because of its specific growth spot. A tree's location—whether in a field, in a valley, or at a southern coordinate versus a northern coordinate—did not matter because that specification was an expendable, circumstantial detail. Irrespective of their circumstances, the trees and plants grew and blossomed solely because of their connection to a life-giving source. And we, as well, can flourish and bear fruit when we are connected to a Life Source—regardless of our circumstances. We will not bear strawberries or any other earthly fruit, but we will yield heavenly fruit from a storehouse, not of this world.

"But the Holy Spirit produces this kind of fruit in our lives: love, joy, peace, patience, kindness, goodness, faithfulness, gentleness, and self-control" (Galatians 5:22-23a, NLT).

Can you imagine the byproducts fruit like that could elicit when shared with others around us? Let alone the byproducts that our own lives could produce? Thank goodness that heavenly fruit is always in season.

Beyond tripping over the fruit on Day Three, we continue to run into the repeated phrase "according to their kinds"— each seed and tree produced only according to its kind. This statement isn't likely to shock you since it's common knowledge that an apple tree cannot produce a peach any more than a hamster can give birth to a puppy. But the phrase warrants repetition because God is establishing an order for the progression of life that He wants us to apply on a deeper level. As the familiar saying goes, it's impossible to play with fire and not get burned. In the same way, you cannot consume junk food as fuel for a bodybuilder physique. Neither can you plant lies in your mind and reap a harvest of healthy truth. Good cannot produce evil, and evil cannot produce good. Each quality follows the scripted order and produces after its kind.

We need a life source to fuel our life, but we must find a trustworthy, good one if we want to produce good things from our life. Jesus took the guesswork out of locating a good life source when He identified Himself as the *true* Vine. With these distinctions, Jesus verified Himself as both a life source and a trustworthy one—just the kind we need to anchor ourselves to!

The problem with lush growth? It requires some space to grow! Yet, before any vegetation had sprouted, God began Day Three by gathering the water to expose the land underneath. God was already working on a solution before we could even recognize a need! Though He had, technically, already supplied the necessary provisions for growth, He had to unearth them from a watery covering before we could see the possibilities.

God simultaneously opened the door to new opportunities by unveiling the new land. Now, there was room to grow, expand our interests, enjoy new activities, and increase production. But wait, that raises another problem with lush growth: What do we do with any surplus? Though it's a shame to waste good food, it's an even further tragedy to waste good fruit in our life. However, these new outlets may allow us to cultivate and glean so much growth that we might find ourselves in abundance. Abundance may mean a valuable talent that could be an invaluable help to someone else. Abundance may look like a few extra minutes to write an encouraging note. Perhaps abundance arises from possessing specialized wisdom and insight that could benefit numerous others. Or maybe an unexpected financial gain allows the extension of funds to meet a need. In any form, a blessing always has room to grow.

We may start as a branch, but God allows us to grab on and branch out.

DAY FOUR: THE RIGHT LIGHT AT THE RIGHT TIME

And God said, "Let there be lights in the vault of the sky to separate the day from the night, and let them serve as signs to mark sacred times, and days and years, and let them be lights in the vault of the sky to give light on the earth." And it was so. God made two great lights—the greater light to govern the day and the lesser light to govern the night. He also made the stars. God set them in the vault of the sky to give light on the earth, to govern the day and the night, and to separate light from darkness. And God saw that it was good. And there was evening, and there was morning—the fourth day.

Genesis 1:14-19

So here we see it again—light, light, and more light! While light on Day One launched with a limited scope, strictly distinguishing between day versus night, on Day Four, that light expanded to include the Sun for the day and the moon and stars for the night. The earth now boasted a vast array of lights that were adjustable for differing seasons and customized for designated times.

We all understand that we cannot categorize our unique stories into a one-size-fits-all box. So we allow for variety within our stories and acknowledge diversity within our needs and hurts. Yet, in some ways, we are the same. Consider the times when our eyes are accustomed to darkness. We all know how it feels to be blinded by light after being asleep or in a dark room for an extended time. At first, a bright light proves too harsh: It shocks our eyes. And what do we do? We cringe. We cover our eyes. We simply cannot adjust that quickly to such a drastic change.

How true that concept reveals itself, too, when we are accustomed to the darkness of our pain—accustomed to the darkness of loneliness, confusion, and sadness. We might need light, but how we apply the light is crucial. It must be done with care. God knows this. He knows all our different seasons and chapters of life. He knows all our days and years—the good and bad. And He knows that pain requires gentleness, so He meets us where we are to tenderly shed light on our pains with His choice of hand-crafted options.

Through our exposure to many lights, we learn to appreciate the appropriate illumination given our specific needs. Then, when we spot a similar condition in someone else, we can select, with pinpoint accuracy, the right light at the right time. What began as God's light shining in our life now reflects to illuminate the world around us. Light, light, and more light equals truth, truth, and more truth. This pattern will naturally lead to healing, healing, and more healing—in our lives and others' lives too.

DAY FIVE: UNITY DONE WELL

And God said, "Let the water teem with living creatures, and let birds fly above the earth across the vault of the sky." So God created the great creatures of the sea and every living thing with which the water teems and that moves about in it, according to their kinds, and every winged bird according to its kind. And God saw that it was good. God blessed them and said, "Be fruitful and increase in number and fill the water in the seas, and let the birds increase on the earth." And there was evening, and there was morning—the fifth day.

Genesis 1:20-23

What a bustle of changes that began on Day Five! We find birds flying through the sky and sea creatures swimming in the deep. God dropped a pebble in the Creation pond, and the creative ripples rolled out! Change after change, and ripple after ripple.

God, once again, demonstrated the ordered progression of life, but on this day, He created sea creatures and birds according to their kinds. In another unique move, God closed Day Five by issuing an order to His newly created animals: Increase in number. Of course, an animal couldn't live in isolation and fulfill that command. So tucked within the command was the awareness that an animal would need to be in community with other animals of its kind to carry out its directive.

Though God kick-started the creative ripples, He asked creation to step up to keep them coming. He didn't call a solo act, and He wasn't interested in humdrum cookie-cutter productions either. So He prescribed countless communities to each gather as a whole in the unified pursuit of a world distinguished by variation. Unity, on this scale, wouldn't achieve multiple results. It would achieve myriad results.

Suppose you toss a single rock into a pond or creek. Despite the satisfaction of hearing a kerplunk and watching the rock generate some impressive surging ripples, your amusement will be short-lived as the surrounding water will quickly restrain the rock's attempted disruption. However, suppose you toss several rocks into the water at once. In that case, you will observe innumerable rows of marching ripples rising and falling, bouncing and overlapping, completely disrupting the surface of the water. These ripples will expand farther and continue longer than the single rock's impact—this is a picture of community.

Please, don't panic, all my fellow introverts! I hear you because I'm right there with you. But whatever our introvert or extrovert wirings, "community" can be used differently. As introverts, our hearts likely race when contemplating community as a group of people, presuming this insinuates an intimidating, large group. While community can imply numbers, it can also refer to a sense of belonging—a companionship among friends. Is it fair to assume that a sense of belonging exists only within an intimidating, large group of people? Not at all. Extroverted individuals, hard-wired to crave all things social, will likely gravitate to more considerable numbers and numerous communities—and, for them, that is great! But when speaking of a sense of belonging, it is just as plausible and accurate to use the word "community," whether referring to one confidante or one hundred.

Wherever you fall on the social spectrum, it would be understandable if your negative experiences have injected some timidity into your relationships. Though we should approach our relationships with discernment, it is equally necessary to maintain some realism in our relationships as well. In our broken world, it is impractical to anticipate finding a perfect individual. Instead of seeking perfection, we should aim for companions who demonstrate support more consistently than disregard or harm.

A healthy community isn't a number but a mindset: Community forms when any number of imperfect human beings believe that life is better experienced together than in isolation. Though community takes an effort to achieve it and poses a risk to engage in it, we simply weren't built to operate independently.

Community increased numbers and boosted variety in the Creation story. It accomplished intensified effects that could span farther and continue longer in the pond analogy. And community works in all the same ways in our personal lives. In seclusion, we could never observe differences nor comprehend their benefits—strengths to offset our weaknesses, resolutions to counter our question marks. We would miss out on a world of variety—a world of creativity meant to add color and life to our existence and our kind. When we find our people, find a person, or add to cherished relationships we have collected along our way, a grouping affords us collaboration for endeavors that would be unattainable on our own. As each individual benefits the larger community, the community, in exchange, fortifies each individual with a sense of belonging.

Unity, when done well, still has a way of making a splash. When people come together, despite any number of possible reasons for division, the world notices. When love supersedes differences, the world does a double take. Unity is still our best option to amplify our efforts and achieve results that ripple larger and longer in the world. Though individuals each leave behind unique remnants of change, their collective changes merge to total a revamped world that is more lively and colorful than ever before.

Unity always leaves behind the aroma of hope. Its fresh air rejuvenates our hope for life in an otherwise empty world. Every time we release its scent, the creation and variety of new life will fill the air and our surroundings again.

DAY SIX: KNOWING OUR AIM

And God said, "Let the land produce living creatures according to their kinds: the livestock, the creatures that move along the ground, and the wild animals, each according to its kind." And it was so. God made the wild animals according to their kinds, the livestock according to their kinds, and all the creatures that move along the ground according to their kinds. And God saw that it was good. Then God said, "Let us make mankind in our image, in our likeness, so that they may rule over the fish in the sea and the birds in the sky, over the livestock and all the wild animals, and over all the creatures that move along the ground." So God created mankind in His own image, in the image of God He created them; male and female He created them. God blessed them and said to them, "*Be fruitful* and *increase in number*; *fill the earth* and subdue it. *Rule* over the fish in the sea and the birds in the sky and over every living creature that moves on the ground." Then God said, "I give you every seed-bearing plant on the face of the whole earth and every tree that has fruit with seed in it. They will be yours for food. And to all the beasts of the earth and all the birds in the sky and all the creatures that move along the ground—everything that has the breath of life in it—I give every green plant for food." And it was so. God saw all that He had made, and it was *very* good. And there was evening, and there was morning—the sixth day.

Genesis 1:24-31, emphasis mine

God's decorative skills were on parade during Day Six. Not only did He fill the earth with all kinds of land animals, but He also created His defining piece of creation: man. To initiate the start of humans filling the earth, God created Adam and then his helper, Eve. And things were not just good—they were *very* good! So to keep things marching in the right direction, He showcased several tasks: Be fruitful! Increase in number! Fill the earth! Rule!

Be fruitful. It's not the exact expression you will likely write on a graduation or wedding card. Nonetheless, God told Adam and Eve to be productive, to produce excellent and helpful results. Likewise, God still asks the same of us today. He charges us to be fruitful—right where He has planted us with our sphere of influence at this distinct moment in history, in our specific location in the world, and among the exact people He has placed us with.

Increase in number—give community a try, even if community means just one other person. Seek collaboration and unity with others to fortify yourself and multiply your results. Unity done well attracts others and, in turn, produces more witness to God's glory.

Fill the earth—not necessarily with more physical lives but with variety. Some variety is easy to appreciate; at other times, differences may prove harder to accept. Yet as we practice our appreciation, thank goodness for a variety of fruit—like peace, patience, kindness, gentleness, and self-control—to go around.

Rule—have control and take charge of God's kingdom and His people. Rise up against the charging enemy, and do not surrender your life to him. As the Creation days proclaim, *God created you for so much more!*

Indeed, God rendered His original creation unstained. Perfect. But humans took little time to muck up His world. The demise started in only the third chapter of the first book of the Bible and continued through all the remaining 65 books and 1,186 chapters that followed.[8]

You see, the Creation story explains our past beginnings, applies to our present stories, and also points to a hopeful world yet to come. God is not teasing us with a story—He is showing us how He wanted things to be and how He is working to put them back together again.

We are not there yet.

But at least we know our aim—how we were created, why we were created, what God is seeking to restore, and how God wants to partner with us to continue creating it according to His design.

5

SEEKING IT

My kids crowned hide-and-seek their favorite household game during their younger years. If they felt extra daring, they would request to play at night using flashlights as their sole tool for sight and seeking. I found this tactic too suspenseful—even as the one hiding!

Perhaps you believe I was attempting to play a game of hide-and-seek with you? Did you notice something was missing?

Good catch! Yes, Day Seven of Creation. The Creation Story always encompasses seven days, not six. So why stop the last chapter one day shy of the complete story? Because I want us to seek. To continue to reveal the hidden messages and applications of Day Seven in our life today—no flashlights needed.

DAY SEVEN: WHEN THE WORK IS DONE

Thus the heavens and the earth were completed in all their vast array. By the seventh day God had finished the work He had been doing; so on the seventh day He rested from all His work. Then God blessed the seventh day and made it holy, because on it He rested from all the work of creating that He had done.

Genesis 2:1-3

Once God finished His work, once He achieved His purposes—then God rested. That seems logical enough. We, too, like to relax and recharge after a long day's work or an exhaustive week. But, we are dealing with human bodies that tire and grow weary. God? He does not grow tired or weary—or even require sleep! So why did He *rest* on the seventh day?

As I hope I have previously shown, we can draw multiple applications from any Bible story and use them for value in our lives today. Some have proposed that God rested on the seventh day as a model for us. This way, by setting aside a day of rest during the week, not only do we benefit ourselves physically and emotionally, but we also bring honor to God by following His example. Pronounced variances exist on what a day of rest implies, and you can decide those technicalities best through your conviction and God's leading.

However, beyond setting an example for us, I believe that God's rest on the seventh day may also point to something else. Something beyond our current days.

God had just finished creating a beautiful, perfect, harmonious world with everything necessary to sustain life and live in harmony with Him. Nothing further was needed. Pleased and content with His work's fruition, God rested.

But we are keenly aware a fall was coming. In the very next chapter of our Genesis story, a fall into sin would fracture this perfect world. Worse yet, a fall into sin was coming that would fracture our ability to have a relationship with God.

We had better return to the story's downward spiral to dig a bit deeper this time. If we continue to the end of the story, we will be in a perfect position to mine some valuable treasures.

Now the serpent was more crafty than any of the wild animals the Lord God had made. He said to the woman, "*Did God really say*, 'You must not eat from any tree in the garden'?"

The woman said to the serpent, "We may eat fruit from the trees in the garden, but God did say, 'You must not eat fruit from the tree that is in the middle of the garden, and you must not touch it, or you will die.'"

"*You will not certainly die*," the serpent said to the woman. "For God knows that when you eat from it your eyes will be opened, and *you will be like God*, knowing good and evil."

When the woman saw that the fruit of the tree was good for food and pleasing to the eye, and also desirable for gaining wisdom, she took some and ate it. She also gave some to her husband, who was with her, and he ate it. Then the eyes of both of them were opened, and they realized they were naked; so they sewed fig leaves together and made coverings for themselves.

Then the man and his wife heard the sound of the Lord God as He was walking in the garden in the cool of the day, and they hid from the Lord God among the trees of the garden. But the Lord God called to the man, "Where are you?"

He answered, "I heard you in the garden, and I was afraid because I was naked; so I hid."

And He [God] said, "Who told you that you were naked? Have you eaten from the tree that I commanded you not to eat from?"

The man said, "The woman you put here with me—she gave me some fruit from the tree, and I ate it."

Then the Lord God said to the woman, "What is this you have done?"

The woman said, "The serpent deceived me, and I ate."

So the Lord God said to the serpent, "Because you have done this, "Cursed are you above all livestock and all wild animals! You will crawl on your belly and you will eat dust all the days of your life. And I will put enmity between you and the woman, and between your offspring and hers; he will crush your head and you will strike his heel."

To the woman He said, "I will make your pains in childbearing very severe; with painful labor you will give birth to children. Your desire will be for your husband, and he will rule over you."

To Adam He said, "Because you listened to your wife and ate fruit from the tree about which I commanded you, 'You must not eat from it,' "Cursed is the ground because of you; through painful toil you will eat food from it all the days of your life. It will produce thorns and thistles for you, and you will eat the plants of the field. By the sweat of your brow you will eat your food until you return to the ground, since from it you were taken; for dust you are and to dust you will return."

Adam named his wife Eve, because she would become the mother of all the living.

The Lord God made garments of skin for Adam and his wife and clothed them. And the Lord God said, "The man has now become like one of us, knowing good and evil. He must not be allowed to reach out his hand and take also from the tree of life and eat, and live forever." So the Lord God banished him from the Garden of Eden to work the ground from which he had been taken. After He drove the man out, He placed on the east side of the Garden of Eden cherubim and a flaming sword flashing back and forth to guard the way to the tree of life.

Genesis 3:1-24, emphasis mine

I'm no archaeologist, but I call that an impressive dig! High five, friend!

Now that we have dug through all the layers of this story, a discovery comes to light: While the majority of the story's participants entered and exited the scenes at irregular intervals, there was one participant, either directly or indirectly, evident in every twist and turn of the story—sin. So given sin's staying power as a dominant role in both ancient history and today's world stage, we would be wise to analyze this character.

If life hands you lemons, by all means, go ahead and make some lemonade. But if a serpent hands you a deadly apple, don't bother looking for apple pie recipes—take aim and throw the apple back! Get rid of the apple as fast as you can—unless. Unless you fell for the bait and have already taken a lethal bite. In that case, you only have one choice: Find an antidote to the apple's poison. (Besides, aim like mine won't get us very far!)

Incredibly, sin has not changed in thousands of years. The repercussions that unfolded in the Creation story can just as readily be exhibited in our lives today. The similarities, though, are worth noting because similar afflictions require similar antidotes. And the sooner you apply an antidote, whether for a deadly apple or a poisonous life, the better!

So to wrap our minds around sin's marked effects, let's get sifting! By my count, we can unearth four main results of sin. But we won't stop there because we need to find some antidotes! So we'll also employ our story diggings to determine God's response to sin's meddling. Within His response, we'll find the necessary remedies.

A TENDENCY TO HIDE

Sin Result # 1: Adam and Eve hid from God.

When approached by God, both Adam and Eve pointed the finger of blame elsewhere: "She made me do it!" or "It was the serpent's fault!"

Ah, ever played the blame game? I certainly have. But it does not matter if we convince ourselves of our innocence. The question remains, does God see it that way? Reading the Bible today, we possess the luxury of knowing the backdrop and the results. So we roll our eyes while lobbing a flippant dig, "Adam and Eve, what royal idiots you were. What an epic fail." An easy thing for us to say, but it's even easier for us to forget that we, too, can wind up in our own abrupt, epic fail. And when failure happens, there's a high probability that we'll choke on our disrespectful words and follow in Adam and Eve's footsteps, hoping to hide from God and hide the truth. But God sees it all. He did not need to ask Adam, "Where are you?" He knew where Adam was. And God did not need to ask Adam if he ate the fruit, for He already knew that answer too.

So why *did* God ask? To show that He had not turned His back on Adam. To show that He still welcomed Adam into a relationship. God allowed Adam the pivotal opportunity to come to Him without force or fear.

Though not a game of hide-and-seek, God came searching. While Adam and Eve were trying to hide, God sought *them*! And God still does that—for me and for you. He still takes the first step. Regardless of where we are or what we have done.

Sin Antidote # 1: While sin inclines us to hide from God, He will always remain available and willing to move toward us if necessary.

DISAPPOINTING SUBSTITUTIONS

Sin Result # 2: Because of sin, painful consequences entered the world.

Physical pain in childbirth. Emotional strain in relationships. Mental frustration in our work.

Now we are relating big time, for those troubles we know full well. The pain, strain, and frustration—all due to sin's arrival.

Simply put, sin is the road that leads to our substitutions for God.

Life submits innumerable roads to obtain material goods, feelings, and relationships. And we head down those roads, hoping that whatever is at the end of the road will fill our empty, longing souls.

Despite what road we take or what object we chase through the consumption of our time, thoughts, and energies—we all share one common outcome. At the end of those roads, we find ourselves still empty. Because the newness wears off, and the anticipation fades every time.

Why does nothing satisfy? How can countless attempts all backfire?

Because a world-shaped peg will never fit in a God-shaped heart.

And everything other than God, no matter what we chase, constitutes a substitution for Him.

Substitutions, by nature, diverge from God's fellowship, His truth, His plan, and His best for us.

How could we allow the enemy to convince us that *anything* could be better than God's best for us?

> *Sin Antidote # 2: We can avoid negative or painful consequences by avoiding inferior substitutions for God.*

CHARACTERISTIC SHAME

Sin Result # 3: Adam and Eve burned with embarrassment when they discovered their nakedness.

Oh, the serpent did say the fruit would open their eyes. It just failed to clarify the change would be for the worse! Please know the enemy's promises never satisfy!

67

By chance, did this sin result hit a nerve for you, too? For I remember the time I found myself naked. I remember the shame and the accompanying hopelessness that arrived with my awareness. And it seems that Adam and Eve felt the same way since their reaction boiled down to running and hiding among the garden trees.

Technically, Adam and Eve had been living naked before being duped by the snake, but they lived in this manner, minus the accompaniment of any embarrassment. Yet when they followed the enemy, he led them straight to shame—the characteristic mark branding his work. And sure enough, after they accepted the enemy's bait, Adam and Eve's self-image collapsed. *God never utilizes embarrassment or shame.*

And God didn't leave Adam and Eve naked, hopeless, or alone either. He covered them—with a literal garment of skins and a figurative garment of grace. He returned them to a state of decency and removed their shame! Adam and Eve's modified state was nothing like God's original design, but don't fail to spot: *God never runs out of options!* He can spin scenarios in ways you and I could never imagine. He can always provide a way back to good—back to Himself.

Sin Antidote # 3: God's job? Removing sin's shame and disgrace. Our job? Merely accepting His grace.

THE PATH BACK TO GOOD

Sin Result # 4: Beyond provoking immediate consequences, sin even generated eternal consequences.

Highlighting verse 22 of Genesis 3, God voiced His concern, "He [man] must not be allowed to reach out his hand and take also from the tree of life and eat, and live forever." God loved humanity too much to pronounce, "You're doomed forever." He had wanted to shield us from a knowledge of evil—*that* would have established our ideal footing. But faced with our shortcomings, He did not want to leave us helpless, forever stuck in the mire of our sin. So He unveiled a new plan in which the poor choice of sin did not have to affect us eternally. He provided us a way out—back onto a path that would lead to *good*. With a master plan to rescue the world through His Son, Jesus, God crushed the devil's game plan.

Drumroll, please.

And the victory goes to...

Not Satan.

Sin Antidote # 4: God is a God of second chances! And third and fourth and fifth! God will not let sin have the final say.

That deserves some fanfare! So yell that "Hallelujah!" Clap your hands, and break out the Happy-Crushing-Satan Dance! Sin will not have the final say! Not in the Creation story—and not in your life or mine!

"But—" you may utter as you slowly stop your happy dance.

But if sin does not have the final say, why do we not always see victory in our lives? Why does sin still have a grip on us? Why do we still agonize with the painful ramifications of sin—daily?

When likening the Creation story to a bigger picture, Day Seven fits into a marvelous spot of that big picture—at the end. As in, the literal end of Earth as we know it: No more pain to feel, sickness to suffer, or death to wrestle.

Once God finished His initial creative work, He rested because He had fulfilled His purposes. And God will end His restoration work in the world today when He fulfills His purpose to gather the most abundant harvest of souls possible. At last, God, His people, and the earth will finally enjoy rest together, and all creation will rightfully be good again!

So you could say that we are essentially living in the Day 6.5 of our parallel, modern Creation story. We have been given a charge and all sustenance for our call. But God's global restoration mission is apparently not completed, for we have yet to witness Day Seven. We still long for the arrival of rest in our world. We still bump into the enemy roaming our Earth and lurking in the shadows of our hearts. And we continue to contend with sin and all its consequences.

But we can find encouragement in the fact that "Jesus Christ is the same yesterday and today and forever" (Hebrews 13:8). That means *God's initial response to sin remains His current response to sin!*

God still meets us where we are with compassion—instead of shaming—and offers us a relationship with Him.

God still initiates our healing from the aftermaths of sin. *God still addresses Satan first.*

Despite their attempt to hide, Adam and Eve's plan flopped. God saw them. However, when faced with God's questions, they eventually came clean. They admitted their sin and awaited their punishment. But God turned to Satan to curse him *first*! Yes, Adam and Eve reaped their fair share of consequences too. Yet, God knows that sin's seed—in any variety—is sown by Satan.

While God will always hate sin, at the same time, He will always love the sinner. If God addresses Satan first when facing sin, we should too!

STILL SEEKING US

So far, since we have maintained an exclusive focus on an individual story in the Bible, we have only begun to skim the surface of the Bible's components. While the Creation story opens the Old Testament, Jesus' arrival on Earth opens the New Testament. Scholars believe that Jesus lived on the earth in a mortal body, susceptible to the same pain, sickness, and emotions as us, for over thirty years. Yet the Bible captures most eyewitness accounts of His thirty years of life and ministry in just four books—the first four books of the New Testament, often called the gospels. These four

SEEKING IT

books detail Jesus' life through only 89 chapters.⁹ Now, I am guessing a lot of you may not have even reached the age of thirty yet, but you are confident that your life history could already fill an awful lot of chapters! So true, I am sure!

Likewise, Jesus' life could have filled untold pages too, for the Bible does not document every story of Jesus' life. The gospels are not a perfect daily diary of Jesus' days. However, they do give us enough information to witness and study Jesus' character—what He stood for and how He lived. Through divine discretion, God provided the highlights He wanted us to have. Thus, every story is even more valuable when we recognize its deliberate selection.

Sometimes, specific Biblical stories can resonate with us more than others or take on new meanings at varying times. But I think the following story will consistently rank as one of my personal favorites, and it begins with Jesus saying,

> "Suppose one of you has a hundred sheep and loses one of them. Doesn't he leave the ninety-nine in the open country and go after the lost sheep until he finds it? And when he finds it, he joyfully puts it on his shoulders and goes home. Then he calls his friends and neighbors together and says, 'Rejoice with me; I have found my lost sheep.' I tell you that in the same way there will be more rejoicing in heaven over one sinner who repents than over ninety-nine righteous persons who do not need to repent. "Or suppose a woman has ten silver coins and loses one. Doesn't she light a lamp, sweep the house and search carefully until she finds it? And when she finds it, she calls her friends and neighbors together and says, 'Rejoice with me; I have found my lost coin.' In the same way, I tell you, there is rejoicing in the presence of the angels of God over one sinner who repents."

> Luke 15:4-10

71

If you doubted it before, I hope this story cements it: *God always seeks us.*

He makes every effort to seek the lost souls the world has tried to cover, bury, or hide—even if that means just one lost soul. He chose to die for you, bleed for you, and give His last earthly breath for you. So you can be assured, He would not hesitate to rescue you, carry you, or love you, for He values your heart above all else.

Shame cannot haunt you anymore because *rejoicing* erupts in heaven for every shame-covered person who turns to meet God's gaze. Celebratory *joy* unleashes when one worn-out person accepts His extended Hand, climbs onto His shoulders, and gets carried to safety. God's goodness is beyond compare, and He will prove it time and time again. The world may look past you to a clamor of ninety-nine others, but God sees you as if you alone stand before Him. And, oh, how He looks through eyes of love!

So if God has given so much to seek us, why not put our hand in His? Why not accept His offer of rescue? God has always been in the business of seeking and saving the lost. Since time began, He has been intent on preparing a way for us to experience a restored life—a life reunited with His heart and His companionship. Why wouldn't we want a life like that?

I think we all need to place a proper emphasis on this intended life, given God's deep regard and investment in it, and I think we should lose no time in running toward it and seeking it for all we are worth.

Right now, we may feel disheartened.

But, by no means are we disqualified.

Right now, we may be fallen, but we are only fallen—not finished.

6

KNOWING IT

"Time heals all wounds."

"It will all work out for the best."

"What doesn't kill you makes you stronger."

"God will only give you as much as you can handle."

S uch statements make me want to gag, barf, or throw a punch. *Or two.*

How often do those heartfelt words of "wisdom" smother a struggling heart? No one has ever accused me of mastering patience—and hearing those words elicit feelings in me that verify my lack of mastery!

We all have experience dealing with someone who thinks they have our life or situation all figured out and finds our answers painfully obvious, our mistakes glaring, and our solution within easy reach. If only we do this, say that, or change these things, we can put our life back together. And though there are times when outside wisdom and unbiased eyes can shed some necessary insight, reality cautions us that not all advice is truthful. Despite their best intentions, others can steer us wrong or even drive us into the ground.

Does misery love company? Perhaps, but sometimes, the company produces misery! Anytime someone spouts empty words or poor clichés, hope goes unheard. Instead, the recipient is left reeling, feeling even lousier than before hearing the proposed encouragement.

STIRRING UP MISERY

To believe the expression "time heals all wounds," we should find a progression toward happiness with each passing year. One should witness nothing but joy by the age of ninety years old, right? But obviously, that is not the case. Instead, physical deterioration, sicknesses, and lost relationships because of tragedy or death only increase with age—no endorsement for healing with time yet. And though time may allow growth or learning opportunities, it certainly makes no promises. If pain is not handled adequately or dealt with in a healthy manner, then pain does not just fade or disappear with time. If anything, time unaccompanied by action will most often cause the hurt to fester, grow, or spread. No, time itself does not heal all pain.

And how about "it will all work out for the best." Will it? Because life is not feeling its best for the woman battling depression. Life is not looking its best for the patient diagnosed with a terminal illness. And hitting close to home, life is not leading to the best interests of the girl or woman living with patterns of sexual destruction. Why is the above expression not true? Because it leads us to believe that we can expect fallen, broken things to give rise to good things. But bad does not inherently produce good. Sin does not partner with the truth. And hurt does not spontaneously heal.

"What doesn't kill you makes you stronger." This expression may be true in a gym setting. Even though the treadmill may feel like a medieval torture device, we can agree that physical training typically produces beneficial changes. Yet, shifting our focus, we confront situations that promote neither our health nor our good. Situations that, instead, harm us because they are rooted in another's selfish desires and, therefore, bring no beneficial effects, physically or emotionally speaking. While a betrayal, coercion, or insult may not kill you, the hidden wounds left by these stealthy attacks can cripple your soul. Despite surviving the damage, you will initially emerge far weaker than prior to your wounding, and the internal damages will remain without proper attention.

And the last phrase, "God will only give you as much as you can handle"—if anyone ever delivered those words to you as consolation for your pain, but, in reality, those words landed a more successful blow to your gut, I want to apologize. Apologize on behalf of, perhaps, the Christian community who uttered those words. Apologize for the condescending punch those words likely landed. And apologize for the poor representation and twisting of God's words. I call it a twisting because no author of any Biblical book ever made that claim or statement. Reading through the Bible, we come toe-to-toe with countless unmanageable, uncontainable troubles without handles!

- Sea waters needing parting
- Unethical rulers
- Murderous plots
- Angry mobs
- Wars
- Giants
- Barren wombs
- Prisons
- Kidnapping
- Rape

- Earthly storms

- Famines

Stop me now because I am just getting started! Who in her right and logical mind could handle even *one* of those situations on her own? You are right—no one. But an actual claim made by the Bible reads, "With man this is impossible, but not *with God*; all things are possible *with God*" (Mark 10:27, emphasis mine). So the ability of anyone to survive an earthly storm, sickness, devastation, or soul-crushing problem of any sort does not speak to any strength of her own. The fact that you and I are still surviving speaks only to the grace of God. Neither you nor I were smart enough or strong enough to get us to this point. How can I say that? Because as we learned back in chapter 4, John 15:5 says, "Apart from Me you can do nothing." Even our very breath is a gift from God. On our own, we utterly lack any ability to control a single facet of our lives. We exist in a world warring against design, reason, and love. No one could do battle alone on this battlefield.

However, God does not create the battlefields we cannot handle—His character forbids Him to promote sin, temptation, or any other evil or harmful act. So God will not give you more than you can handle, but you can be sure that this broken world will give you more than you can handle on your own!

JOB'S APPARENT TROUBLE

A book in the Bible that is often most dear to those struggling with suffering is the book of Job. Yet, when we first meet Job, he seems like the all-around "man." He is rich, powerful, happy, and successful. During his time, the economy centered on agriculture, and Job amassed wealth because of his abundant supply of livestock, land, and buildings. Besides material assets, Job also enjoyed a blessed family life. As a happily married man, he looked after his children and watched them grow into successful, happy adults.

Although Job's life, in the early stages, rivals a Disney® story, his fairy tale takes a sharp, downward turn when another person slinks onto the scene. One who already had a prominent run in the Creation story but refused to be limited to fifteen minutes of fame!

> The Lord said to Satan, "Where have you come from?"
>
> Satan answered the Lord, "From roaming throughout the earth, going back and forth on it."
>
> Then the Lord said to Satan, "Have you considered my servant Job? There is no one on earth like him; he is blameless and upright, a man who fears God and shuns evil."
>
> "Does Job fear God for nothing?" Satan replied. "Have You not put a hedge around him and his household and everything he has? You have blessed the work of his hands, so that his flocks and herds are spread throughout the land. But now stretch out Your hand and strike everything he has, and he will surely curse You to Your face."
>
> The Lord said to Satan, "Very well, then, everything he has is in your power, but on the man himself do not lay a finger."
>
> Job 1:7-12

At this point, we can recognize an all-too-familiar enemy. One who is always roaming, looking to devour or destroy. This time, Satan attempted to exterminate Job's faith to make a fool of God. *But every time, Satan always aims to remove witness, glory, and hearts from the Lord.*

In *one* day, through a series of freak catastrophes, Job lost all his livestock, fields, buildings, and children. His life's work—obliterated. After these devastations, three of Job's friends came to him and tried their best to console him. While their efforts seem admirable at first, their solace matched the likes of the advice at this chapter's start—you know, the advice that made me hurl. For they aired the presumptuous counsel, "Those who plow evil and those who sow trouble reap it" (Job 4:8). Talk about a slap in the face! With rapid-fire succession, those friends took turns lobbying chastisements and corrections at Job. They scrutinized Job's life and had it "all figured out" with ease. From their arrogance, they were unafraid to boast solutions and detail every error that *must* have brought Job to this dismal outcome. They proposed the flippant formula: Do this, and you will have no more troubles.

But the book of Job dispenses vital information to its readers in the very first verse! Job 1:1 reads, "In the land of Uz there lived a man whose name was Job. *This man was blameless and upright; he feared God and shunned evil*" (emphasis mine). According to Job's friends, suffering signified a merited punishment. They concluded, "If you are having troubles or find yourself over your head, well, you must have done something wrong." In all likelihood, they arrived at this deduction by the memory of a mess brought on by their *own* doing, and no doubt, we can all appreciate the embarrassment of creating a mess.

DUMB CALLS AND DUMBER INJUSTICE

One time when my brother was around four years old, my mom noticed him huddled on the floor underneath a rocking chair in his room. When she entered his room, he scrambled to his feet, appearing equally startled and guilty. My mom noticed an empty foil wrapper on the floor and asked him, "Were you eating this?" My brother, gaining his composure, flat-out denied the accusation. However, he missed that a comic piece of evidence proclaimed otherwise. It just so happened the foil wrapper contained little red medicine tablets that a child could have mistaken for candy. Regardless of the pills' attraction, my brother was adamant about his innocence while unknowingly sporting red, splotchy stains around his mouth! Maneuvering around my brother's growing nose, my mom placed an urgent phone call to Poison Control, who prescribed medicine to induce vomiting and rid his system of the pills. Yep. Dumb calls. Dumb results. Been there, done that.

And yet, when we think of a time that we messed up and suffered a consequence, even though we don't rate the experience as enjoyable, we find it easier to come to grips with an outcome resulting from an identifiable error. When we incur suffering as a result of our own doing, we only have ourselves to blame. Therefore, we find it a bit easier to accept the subsequent consequence as fitting and just, and that logic somewhat calms our disappointment or frustration.

However, what can exhaust or surpass our patience—at least the patience-challenged folks like me—are unmerited hardships: when we face frustrations *without* committing any prior error or unwise step. When others accuse us of doing or saying something we did not, penalize us for someone else's shortcomings, tag us with a cruel label, exclude us because of our skin color, or judge us by a family member's reputation— you name it. Unmerited suffering strikes us as so *unjust*, and our souls long for justice. We long to see the good guys win and the bad guys lose.

Yet, despite our innate desire for justice, we trend toward two unfortunate tendencies in matters involving suffering. First, we only seem to entertain the possibility of unjustified suffering when we are the ones suffering. And second, as the friends in Job illustrate, we are often inclined to display a prideful tendency when we find ourselves on the other side of suffering—not in the hot seat. Clouded judgment can tempt us to pass quick diagnoses, see others' situations as black and white, and presume their suffering results from of a wrong action.

But, again, the first verse of Job grants no liberty to make any assumptions in Job's case because it emphasizes that Job was "blameless and upright." On top of that, it also directly points out that Job has "forsaken evil." No just punishment going on here. Indeed, none of the tragedies in Job's life connected to any poor call on his part, yet, they occurred nonetheless.

And while I wish for Job's sake that this point marked his misery's extent, hardship continued to pummel him. Job later lost his health, and his body withered from the abuse of both mental and physical pain. His sickness rendered him almost unrecognizable to his friends and reduced him to scraping his sores with a broken piece of pottery while he sat on the ground and pondered his life. Job's fairy tale? Bibbidi-bobbidi-poof. Gone. His world had thoroughly shattered, and his life had imploded. Exacerbating the situation, Job had to further contend with the condescending, faulty judgments of his friends who made a sport out of dumping salt into his wounds.

BUT, WHY NOT FIX IT?

Understandably, Job wondered why he was ever born if his life would only amount to disaster and sorrow. You may have pondered that same question about your life.

Why, God? *Why?*

Why allow Satan to induce all this hurt and pain? Why not take this circumstance out of my hands? Why not remove these people from my life? Why not protect me from all this? Why, why, why?

I would love the pleasure of pinpointing a verse or chapter in Job to provide a concise, quick answer to all of your "whys." And please believe the ache in my heart as I say that because I also sought the very same thing. But I have found that our quest for answers will require searching beyond just a single verse or chapter in the Bible, for the Bible gathers an assortment of individual story strands and weaves them together, ultimately assembling a complex tapestry. This tapestry exhibits testimony to a Masterful Weaver—One who can take the dark sections and incorporate them smack dab into a bright portion. One who does not waste any pieces or parts but can find a place and a purpose for everything. Even the thing the enemy had fashioned to harm us, God can repurpose to deliver a victory. So I don't think we should hope to appease ourselves with a single Bible verse or chapter because God leverages vast storehouses of comfort. A quick fix sums up the meager solution we humanly look for—what Job's friends attempted with their narrow insight. Yet it's easy to forgive a world that often swoops in to manufacture an explanation or concoct an escape from pain and suffering, for we get it: People cook up plans and come up with clever catchphrases or witty advice to apply a Band-Aid® at the moment because hurting hearts are desperate for something—anything—to help them get by.

But this Creator, this Designer I have been presenting, does not work in such an abrupt manner. The precepts of His character will not allow Him to suggest an explanation detached from His heart, and herein lies the problem with the shortcuts we try to take in our own lives or in analyzing someone else's life. We look to sentiments that, even if they have truth, might lack heart—a heart to enter the pain and comprehend the whole situation. If actions speak louder than words, perhaps the loudest support we could ever express to someone wouldn't require our words but some of our time to sit in their pain with them—in silence, realizing that words can sometimes fall flat.

Yet relationship never will.

This principle forms the foundation of God's prescription for our pain: No quick passing words of consolation, but a relationship that enters our pain.

Why not simply take the pain away, you wonder? I must admit, that question poses a profound mystery. Plenty of scholars, renowned individuals, and everyday people ask that exact same question as well. Removing us from our trouble strikes us as the most logical and immediate solution, so we find it impossible to resist asking, "Why not?" Yet, on this side of heaven, I wonder if we could fathom our question's answer. But through all my years of questioning, I humbly submit the following as the strongest argument that I can suggest:

Impairing an injury disables the opportunity for healing.

Pacifying the pain stifles the craving for peace.

Erasing darkness wipes out the appreciation for light.

Ending brokenness and sin halts the righteous anger that fuels our yearning for a better option.

If we could live in a self-sufficient manner, what would we ever need? Obviously, nothing. And though we try to delude ourselves with visions of self-sufficiency because we fear depending on anything or anyone, the evident fact remains: God created us to need one remarkably big thing—Him.

All of our pains—in any form—accentuate an intense awareness of our insufficiency and prod us to seek better options. Only when looking for answers can we find *the* Answer—help for today and, as a surprising bonus, help for eternity.

COUNTERING UNPLEASANT PAIN

Have you noticed that when a healthy relationship of friendship or love is present in your life, your location or choice of activities doesn't matter? Whether plummeting on a roller coaster or biking up a hill, you feel only bliss because the relationship alone is enough to satisfy and fill your heart. Building on that example, imagine a relationship with God bringing the same fulfillment—only on a whole new level of bliss and joy. For God fills you with the kind of love that sustains joy in the face of pain. Peace in the face of suffering.

So while God does not create the pain or the brokenness in this world, He allows us to live in it even though He fully acknowledges the severity of the brokenness. But rather than eliminate the bad in our lives, He uses it as a catalyst to expose our need for the healing and love that only He can provide. And when you know His love and experience a relationship with Him, the rest fades in comparison. Whether enjoying the view from a mountain peak or enduring a fierce storm in your life, your focus settles on your Companion instead of your location.

Now, humanly speaking, I am not suggesting that we will ever enjoy pain. And in our humanity, we can expect some questions to persist in our minds. But our questions do not irritate God, and He does not demand the absence of all doubt. Quite the opposite, He welcomes our willingness to be open with Him because honesty paves the only avenue leading to a healthy, growing relationship.

I cringe to admit it, yet something about pain fashions a unique effect on our hearts and souls and leads us to a desperate place of searching and longing like nothing else. For your sake and mine, I wish we could learn better through an alternative method! But pain remains our most efficient motivation for beelining to the end of our rope, where we will land in a classroom for master's level courses in rawness, brokenness, and surrender. Upon completing these rigorous courses, our experience will afford us a license in either empathy or bitterness—the two specialized fields of pain to choose from.

While I would never claim to grasp the mind of God, I am confident that God does *not* enjoy our suffering any more than we do. In fact, the Bible describes Jesus as God's representative—a mirror image reflecting the person of God, allowing us to see what human eyes cannot perceive. Above all, Jesus came to Earth to save us from our sins and to provide us the chance for a renewed life as He had desired. But He could have accomplished that mission in one day. It's true: As horrific as Jesus' crucifixion was, it took place in the time frame of one day. So why not come to Earth, suffer the cross as quickly as possible, and call it a day? Why did Jesus choose to enter the world as a helpless baby instead? Why did He prefer to experience the trials and tribulations of growing up and living through all the agonies and challenges of everyday life, twenty-four-seven, for over thirty years?

Why? To confirm that He is not unwilling nor afraid to enter our pain.

To pledge that He is a trustworthy friend. A friend who can introduce true consolation and comfort because He fully empathizes with our hurts.

Isaiah 53:3 says, "He was despised and rejected by mankind, a man of suffering, and *familiar with pain*" (emphasis mine).

I take that verse to heart whenever I find myself in a valley. I consider, *How can Jesus understand my emotions? What did He experience that parallels what I am encountering?*

And if we investigate His time on Earth, we will find assurance that He does indeed understand all our suffering.

Do you feel rejected? Jesus' own people rejected Him. Lonely? He faced all kinds of trials without support. Uncelebrated and unrecognized? A myriad of people despised and ignored Him. Betrayed? Check. Wounds from family or friends? A few of those closest to Him belittled and used Him, too. Whatever the world may call Jesus, it cannot call Him a stranger to suffering.

BEYOND FORMALITIES

And speaking of suffering, what ever happened to our poor guy Job? Though God did not give Job specific answers to his questions about suffering, God did not stay silent either. Yet Job could only process astonishment as, one by one, God dismantled Job's questions with His own inquiries. God asked Job if he was present at the spreading of the heavens or the fashioning of the earth. He investigated whether Job knew how the dawn appeared or how to halt the ocean's waves. God also quizzed Job about where the flowers and animals received their wisdom.

What could Job say? Unable to Google for the next several thousand years, Job took a hard pass.

Job realized that he had no right to question God's ways or to assume that he possessed the wisdom to comprehend God's ways. But God was generous and did not end the conversation there. In His kindness, He vindicated Job from the judgments of his friends. God spoke to the three friends and told them He was angry with them "because you have not spoken truth about Me, as My servant Job has" (Job 42:7b). God instructed the friends to offer sacrifices of atonement for the wrongs they had spoken to Job. And then—catch this—God asked Job to *pray* for his friends.

Another twist in the story, right? For if Job had done no wrong, remained faithful through loss, and earned God's continued confirmation throughout the drawn-out conflict with his friends, why did God ask Job to pray for his friends?

Well, I believe this request allows us a privileged glimpse into the heart of God. Considering the story's events, we can deduce that social status did not impress God. Long-winded wisdom did not move Him. Even the act of sacrifice did not guarantee God's pleasure. *But God was and will always be intent on harvesting hearts.* God knew that mindless, routine compliance or a checkmark on a to-do list could not satisfy His request. Job would have to push beyond formalities.

Our human nature looks forward to Job taking his friends' noses, rubbing them in his affirmation from God, and finishing with a spiteful "Told you so!" dripping with attitude. But instead, Job set aside his pride and agenda and prayed for his friends.

Through his response, Job subjected his heart to a litmus test: What was the condition of his heart? The test result indicated that Job had bonded his heart with God's, for how else could Job have prayed for—rather than cursed—those who had wronged him? In the end, God's request exposed whether Job would prefer to indulge God's heart or his own sinful heart. Job chose wisely because he did not value the world's opinion as much as he valued God's approval.

CONSIDERING FORGIVENESS

How could Job have set aside his natural desire for justice to summon the willingness or strength to pray for his less-than-friendly companions? And to put it personally, how could you or I ever pray for the very ones who have hurt us? Well, here are the three transformative thoughts that have enabled me to gain ground in my ongoing process of choosing forgiveness.

First, I remember my proper starting point: below God. Before his suffering, Job *knew of* God. But it wasn't until he walked through suffering that Job *knew* God and appreciated a deep-seated wonder of Him. And as Job piled up the wonders—God alone qualified as holy, God alone possessed all knowledge, and God alone held all of time—he was overwhelmed by the realization that *he* could no longer claim to be the one who was offended. Since God dictated the standard of good, set the measure of perfection, ran the world, and penned the rules, any offense ultimately fell against *Him*.

In the same way, we perceive offenses as ours to hold when the truth is we should pass them along to their reassigned, rightful Owner. A proper starting point requires us to remove ourselves as the focal point of our world and allow God to assume His merited spot on the throne of our hearts. When His rights own first place, our desires and longings occupy second place—and priorities shift. We do not have to consume ourselves with quests of retribution, vengeance, or even gaining approval solely for the sake of our pride, for we are not ultimately due those things. You can remove the heavy burden of justice from your shoulders and just breathe. Let God own the wrongs—and the entitlement to right those wrongs.

Second, God never asked Job to dismiss the pain that came into his life or get over the hurtful things his friends said. What a relief that God will never ask us to shrug off our pain, either. Instead, God allows us the right to grieve and hurt. Again, He, too, tasted sorrow while in our world. Though it's hard for us to fathom, brokenness and sin break God's heart more than they will ever break ours. We forget that sin cost God too. God watched His only Son suffer mistreatment and torture to become an atoning sacrifice for those evils. But even God had to look away as the sum weight of sin, from all of time, was transferred to His Son. *Because God despises sin too.* Sin creates a chasm—a divide—between God and us.

But we should not let someone else's sin separate us from God or the life He calls us to. A life that forgives rather than grows in hatred. A life that takes hurt and sin and chooses to place them at the foot of the cross rather than at the front of our minds. If we can realize that no earthly means exist to undo the past and accept that no earthly action, either on our part or another's, can make up for the past, then we can trade our burdened hearts for a lightened load. While forgiveness often requires multiple or daily releasing on our part, it's a favorable alternative to reliving the hurt day after day. *The priority God places on our need to heal spurs His emphasis on our need to forgive*, for He fully comprehends what the reality and brutality of our pain causes. Not for a moment does God ask us to deny our pain, but He does ask us to release the pain to Him so He can tend to our wounds. His bandaging reminds us that God does not take sin lightly, and one day, justice will reign in every respect.

Third, before we can ever process the hurt, we have to identify the source of the hurt. Leading up to this realization, it wasn't unusual for me to numb my pain with a man's presence. But since this technique never cured my hurt, I eventually sought a counselor's help. Through an exercise, my counselor challenged me to speak to God about my pain, ask for healing, and, afterward, listen to see if I could hear from Him. Honestly, I did not approach this task with any hopeful anticipation as I felt I had already tried those steps hundreds of times before. But I honored my counselor's request and tried one more time. And despite my cynical soul, my life forever changed that day.

I began by closing my eyes for the sake of concentration, but then, I proceeded to wrestle. With complete honesty, I bared my soul. I reminded God of the magnitude of my hurt, pleaded for relief from the grief overwhelming my soul, lamented my inability to find love—

But He stopped me, dead in my tracks. And He spoke to me. Not in an audible voice, but ever so clearly in my mind and heart, I heard Him say eight words that would rock my life to its core: *"Love didn't do this to you. Sin did."*

Boom! Mic drop. The end.

What? *Love* did not do this to me? Sin did? The thought floored me for several moments until the truth and beauty of what He said reached the bleeding cracks of my heart. My experiences did *not* involve love. No wonder they hurt, no wonder they did not fulfill. All the pain was *not* due to love. Love was not responsible for my misery. *Sin* was. *Sin caused the breaking, the harming, and the wounding—not love.*

With eight words, decades of pain received intensive care, and my heart began to heal and mend. What difference separates the eight words I heard from the so-called encouragements at the start of the chapter? One ginormous difference: truth. Nowhere near empty, those eight words cut through my presumptions and identified the true source of my pain.

The source of my hurt was not a human, as I had believed, but sin.

I pray these words of truth will blow open the doors of your heart today and revolutionize your life as they did mine. Whether your hurt came at the hands of another person in your life or at the expense of some poor judgments you made, the ultimate source of your hurt is sin.

Knowing now that sin bears the blame for all our pain, why would we continue to run toward sin through more poor choices? Whether we run to the same paths that fail to satisfy us or run from forgiveness, sin compounded with more sin just amounts to bigger messes and deeper hurts. So why not take a step back from your norm and try a step toward forgiveness, either of yourself or another, as need be?

Forgiveness does not mean what has happened in your life no longer matters or is acceptable. And it does not mean that you will receive a rare amnesia to erase all your pain. But God asks us to forgive because He knows forgiveness is our only defensive move to break free from sin's restraint. Sinful experiences that were damaging enough at first can persist to suffocate us when our memory gets stuck on repeat. We rehearse the hurt and exhaust ourselves by grasping, in vain, for some sort of justice or compensation. Forgiveness, however, allows us to lay down the cumbersome chains of memories and hurts we have been dragging. We surrender what we held as our rights to recognize God as the ultimate owner of justice—trusting His ability over ours to settle justice. He might not remove the pain, but He *will* enter the pain with you. And His presence makes all the difference.

Finding the Lost and Retrieving the Stolen

Job's obedience never went unnoticed—ever—throughout his entire story.

"After Job had prayed for his friends, the Lord restored his fortunes and gave him twice as much as he had before. The Lord blessed the latter part of Job's life more than the former part" (Job 42:10, 12a).

God replaced all that was taken from Job's life—and more.

And I believe He wants to do the same for you.

Don't miss this: Nothing has been taken from you that cannot be restored to you when God enters the situation!

More than a mild opposition to the louder messages blasting from society, this message obliterates any belief keeping you from complete redemption. No matter what you've convinced yourself, whether you believe someone or something has ruined you, see no way back, identify no fix, or see your purity as forever lost, this message can trump any rationalization or objection you raise!

It's also able to take on a crowd too. Because maybe it's not yourself you want to convince but others whose reaction you fear or whose discrimination you've already met up with. An unfortunate possibility is that you are apprehensive about a Christian circle with a propensity to promote abstinence louder than the possibility for redemption when abstinence is not the case. *But rising above the noise is an overwhelming, booming, revolutionary truth that stands unshakeable against any opinion or popular vote: You have lost nothing that God's grace cannot restore.*

We find ourselves locking horns with an enemy. But as we look into his eyes, we see the faint flicker of fear reminding us our enemy lacks supremacy. For our enemy can do nothing to us apart from the watchful eye of our Protector. And our Protector oversees like no one else we have ever known. He chases dirtiness away. Cancels any condemning charge. Restores the robbed, innocent pieces. And He unveils the source of our hurt so we can target our enemy. "Then you will know the truth, and the truth will set you free" (John 8:32).

Truth has arrived on the scene.

And knowing it, we find a game changer.

Sin is to blame.

Sin is to blame.

So run to God.

Run to His comfort.

Experience a new beginning.

Your stolen footing? Recovered.

Your chains of guilt? Every pathetic link snapped and lying in a crumpled heap at your feet.

And since your chains are gone, why wait?

Now is finally your chance to experience freedom.

PART 3

THE REWRITE

7
QUITTING IT

Quality is not an act, it is a habit.

—Aristotle

The journey of a thousand miles begins with one step.

—Lao Tzu

You quit. You know why you quit? Because you're a quitter. And everybody knows that quitters, quit.

—Vice Principal Murney in *The Pacifier*

More often than not, in our society, people judge our character as weak or flawed when we display an affinity for giving up on pursuits. The label "quitter" does not garner an ounce of praise. And while success often demands far more effort than giving up, sometimes success requires quitting. Let me elaborate.

Quitting some practices, such as smoking, drugs, or an unhealthy eating pattern, can trigger healthy and applauded results. Halting any of these habits would lead to noticeable improvements in one's physical being, and we could calculate and witness the benefits of quitting.

But of equal importance to our physical health is our emotional health. Although our emotions do not appear as tangible, visible pieces of our being, they carry no less significance to our health. Indeed, scientists have linked negative emotions and stress to depression, sickness, and even death. Dying of a broken heart can be more than just an expression.

Since you have stuck with me this far, I hope you have already begun to uncover and diagnose any unhealthy emotional patterns that have led you to this book. Sexual brokenness runs deep and spreads to unlimited places in our souls. Considering our stories, sin has manipulated and distorted the most intimate act that our bodies and minds can engage in. The mutation remaining from our experiences may not be evident on the surface, and we may not be able to weigh or measure its marks in any way. But make no mistake. Sexual brokenness leaves a wake of bleeding, gaping souls.

Whether you handed over your innocence or someone took it, your loss involved sinful choices by either you or someone else. In both cases, though, the word "choice" implies other options or alternatives existed. While we cannot assume responsibility for the decisions or actions of others, we have to accept responsibility for our choices.

PUTTING IT INTO PLAY

If you're like me, you might be saying, "Okay, I'm on board with this logic, but *how* do I put it into play? What does this look like in real life? How can these thoughts transfer from words on a page into my everyday life?" While these questions warrant an answer, any attempt to supply a one-answer-fits-all is doomed to fail. Quitting the cycles and habits that have brought you to this book will look different for each person, but let me give you a few examples and pictures of how these pieces can connect and play out.

First, if you live in the dangers of sex trafficking, incest, or abuse, I pray that you stake your life in the power of Jesus and that, with just the mere utterance of Jesus' name, your enemy's knees bow in unchallengeable surrender. May your senses be alert to prison doors opening while your enemy's senses dull to this reality. I pray you could pile up memories of Jesus proving Himself stronger than the powers of hell in your life. May He illuminate a pathway leading to trustworthy individuals who could assist you with a plan for safety and guide you to a place of refuge. May you place yourself in His hands, so He can equip you with the tools and means necessary to reorient your life. And with every decision and step you make, I pray His blood covers and protects you from all evil at every turn.

Second, if your life is on a downward spiral due to your habits or actions, a choice will be required. Will you quit, or will you continue? Neither option leads to a carefree solution. Continuing will lead to more of what you already know— perpetual emptiness. But quitting promises difficulty as well. You might sustain the death of a relationship or the end of a dream. New habits form over time, but I promise you that change *is* possible. After some practice and tweaking, your radar will become better attuned to detect the triggers and temptations you would have previously missed.

So as the journey of a thousand miles must begin with one step, the journey to shift your life's direction will also start with one step. Followed by another step. And then one more.

I venture to say that most of us would gravitate to the thrill of a destination over the dullness of a journey. Small steps do not tend to impress us. Hands down, we would all choose to travel at warp speed any day of the week rather than wait on a slower form of travel. Zero effort, zero traffic. Just—boom— you have arrived! But, sadly, science fiction transportation is just that: an imaginary option not available in travel or life. Therefore, we can't hope to pull off a short commute— let alone a relocation of our life—through lightning-fast or temporary adjustments. While you may need to apply some urgent changes for your immediate safety, you will reorient your life only through less than thrilling, day-by-day, and moment-by-moment choices.

Personally, I would like to make my life choices with the advantage of a projected, detailed route to my destination. Sharp right turn, here! Veer left, now! Yes, I will take all the warnings, hints, and a step-by-step structured plan before I begin my journey, please! But life, God, and faith do not grant these luxuries. Faith is required only in the presence of doubt—when we do not have experience on our side, a road map in our hand, or are forced to navigate by unconventional methods because our digital lady friend from the map app needs to recharge.

TRANSFORMING OUR CHOICES

It's fair to compare life to a road trip minus a map or a plan. On a large scale, you expect to navigate several significant, course-altering decisions over your lifetime. But when those decisions will arise or what they entail is yet to be determined. Even on a smaller scale, countless daily decisions threaten to bombard and overwhelm you until you feel incapable of tackling even a minor course of action. By placing extreme importance on each and every step, we constantly live in fear of choosing the wrong one.

Life makes matters worse by throwing in plenty of unforeseen roadblocks and delays as well. (Deep breath, anyone? Just me?) Yet, a sermon I once heard on God's will proposed an alternative outlook on life's choices.

I used to view God's will as an elusive road map that required specific, unalterable turns and roads. I was under the impression that if I veered off the specified path even slightly—wham! Endgame and I hopped on the fast track to nowhere. Yikes, right? No wonder life terrified me.

Is "terrifying" an appropriate description to summarize your take on God's will too? Well, enter a wise sermon to volunteer the following insight: What if God's will resembles a canvas more than a road map? What if flexibility is an option, and creativity is not discouraged?

In the 1980s, a television painting show grew wildly famous thanks to its male star. While this man's painting showcased his undeniable skill, the more admirable draw of his show was his encouraging approach to painting—and life. During any of his shows, Bob Ross never painted a color splotch he could not undo or had a meltdown believing that he had somehow ruined his masterpiece. Nope. Instead, Bob Ross had a habit of assuring his viewers, "There are no mistakes, only happy accidents."[10] As proof, during any of his shows, you could watch him transform dots into a tree's crown or piece together smudges and strokes into a turbulent ocean. His words revealed his belief in the ability to redeem choices: "Mix up a little more shadow color here, then we can put us a little shadow right in there. See how you can move things around? You have unlimited power on this canvas—can literally, literally move mountains."[11]

Bob Ross was not intimidated by a blank canvas. Why? Because he knew who held the paintbrush and chose its course. And he lived from the assurance that second, third, fourth, and future tries were okay because, eventually, a mountain *could* move.

Now, what if you could view your life as that canvas? With the allowance to paint over or transform the parts already started? See a mistake as something other than a mistake? Transform *that* mark into something better?

My heart breaks as I know what some of you are thinking right now—the nagging whispers berating your ears:

Why?

Why bother quitting or changing?

What good will it really do now?

What's done is done.

There is no hope.

You are already ruined.

Scary, right? Like I am reading your mind? Let me resolve your suspicion: I am no mind reader. Any similarities in our thoughts confirm that we have a common enemy resorting to a predictable MO. I know what you are hearing because I have listened to that voice, too: the one discouraging any step toward health or healing and zapping any hope. The voice that always deters, "No way, not possible."

Not possible? Well, while I could continue talking about possibilities, I think it's time to *show* you. Toss out a couple of how-this-looks-in-real-life pictures instead.

PICTURE RAHAB

My first picture captures a woman named Rahab. At first glance, the blurry image might frustrate you because it obscures any distinguishing features of Rahab. But even so, you only need to know one detail about her, for even the citizens of Rahab's town used just one attribute to identify her—her vocation. Rahab was a prostitute. Everyone dismissed her on the grounds of her lack of distinction. Most avoided eye contact as they walked by her. And no one held their breath to hear the roar of heaven's applause for Rahab. But heaven saw fit to present her a choice.

One night, Rahab received two male visitors to her house. But these men were not regular, local guests. They were spies! And when word of the men's visit reached the king, he sent his guards to question Rahab about the spies' whereabouts. With an air of indifference, Rahab explained that the visitors had stopped at her house earlier but had left already. However, she suggested they might catch up with the spies if they hurried. So the king's men took off immediately, but their search amounted to a wild goose chase. For they had been duped by the art of misdirection.

Peeking out her window, Rahab watched as the guards raced away and faded from sight. She couldn't help but smile because her plan had worked brilliantly. She closed her curtain and proceeded to climb up to her rooftop, where she had hidden the spies.

What was Rahab thinking? Lying to the king? Thwarting his men's efforts? Rahab was clearly playing with fire! That is, *if* she did not fear something more powerful than the king. But Rahab possessed a greater appreciation of these secret spies than one might guess.

> And [she] said to them, "I know that the Lord has given you this land and that a great fear of you has fallen on us, so that all who live in this country are melting in fear because of you. We have heard how the Lord dried up the water of the Red Sea for you when you came out of Egypt…. When we heard of it, our hearts melted in fear and everyone's courage failed because of you, for the Lord your God is God in heaven above and on the earth below."
>
> Joshua 2:9-11

Rahab knew that the king had nothing on these guys. Though accustomed to the cruelty of public opinion, Rahab refused to hinge her life on the past or a crummy title. She took advantage of her choice and followed the ultimate King. In turn, the Israelite spies repaid Rahab for her protection by sparing Rahab and her entire family—her mother and father, sisters and brothers, and their families—from the coming attack on their town. Her choice equaled life. Literally, but it meant a whole lot more as well.

When Rahab crossed paths with the two Israelite men, she could never have known the ramifications of that day. She would never have predicted that people would read her captured words thousands of years later, for Rahab could not see the part she was playing in history and had no hunch that she was helping advance God's kingdom on Earth. In a culture that did not deem women equal to men, no one expected a heroine, least of all Rahab! But God was prepared to hand over an MVP accolade that would clinch Rahab's place in the History Makers' Hall of Fame.

While the culture traced genealogy solely through male ancestors, Jesus' lineage, as given in the first chapter of the book of Matthew, took an unusual approach and included the names of five women. One of the women listed was Jesus' mother, Mary, and out of only four other honored spots, Rahab's name made the cut! A rare female selection for any lineage, let alone Jesus' line—and a woman lacking any esteemed credentials, no less. An overlooked and undervalued woman until God entered the scene of her life. Just a typical day until God changed everything.

One ordinary day, one choice—in the hands of a limitless God, becomes a legacy.

Although we celebrate her story, Rahab did not know what history would hold. She never got to see the extended impact of her choice. The only evidence Rahab would have witnessed was the protection of her parents and siblings: a fact for which, I am positive, she was incredibly grateful! But did she ever outlive the title "Rahab the prostitute?" Did others ever hear of her courage or begin to show her some respect in her lifetime? The Bible does not tell us.

But the details of Rahab's life that we *are* given all point to a God who would assure you that your potential isn't determined by what others think of you. It's not even defined by what you think of yourself! Where you came from or what you have done, do not alter it. Your story revolves around what *He* can do for you—and through you.

NOW PRESENTING HAGAR

But I still hold one more picture in my hand. So now I present to you my photograph of Hagar, a servant to a woman named Sarah. Unable to have children, Sarah put a rush on her situation by giving Hagar to her husband, Abraham, to conceive a child for him. Sarah's plan was not a novel idea as masters often did sleep with their servants during these days, yet the commonness of a practice does not provide a defense for its justifiability, neither then nor now. In a situation that boiled down to a forced sexual act for the sole benefit of an employer, Hagar's story could be considered an ancient parallel to present-day sex trafficking. However, Hagar followed orders and did, indeed, conceive a child with Abraham. The successful pregnancy evidently spawned a sense of pride in Hagar because Hagar began to treat Sarah with an air of condescension, adding insult to injury. Jealousy overtook Sarah and even incited her to blame Abraham for what had been her idea! Exasperated by Sarah's complaints, Abraham allowed Sarah to deal with Hagar however she pleased. Sarah hopped on the chance and treated Hagar with such contempt that Hagar felt being pregnant, alone, and on the run would be preferable to Sarah's vengeance. So Hagar packed her bags and fled.

But during her escape, an angel of the Lord visited Hagar. The angel asked her where she was going, and Hagar explained her flight from Sarah. The angel told Hagar that she should return to Sarah, yet he eased the request with a comfort. He told her, "You are now pregnant and you will give birth to a son. You shall name him Ishmael, for the Lord has heard of your misery" (Genesis 16:11).

The angel's appearance may have been a surprise to Hagar's itinerary, but God's attention was a surprise to her heart. A special messenger—just for her? "She gave this name to the Lord who spoke to her: 'You are the God who sees me,' for she said, 'I have now seen the One who sees me'" (Genesis 16:13). Hagar—though used, unloved, and unwanted in the world—now basked in the gaze of the God who actually *saw* her and meticulously cared for the details of her life!

Invisible to others. But *never* to God.

TRADING TRADITION

God still demonstrates a tendency to visit us: smack in our mess and right in the middle of the ordinary! He shows up and establishes He is the God who still sees. Page after page, the Bible deluges us with stories of God showing up. Not running away. Not scared by our current circumstances. On the contrary, He prefers to focus on the lost. The marginalized. The weak. The sick. The outcast.

Jesus touched the lepers. Spoke with the criminals. Ate meals with the outcasts. Called the overlooked near. Instead of looking the other way, He locked eyes with people with disabilities. He traded tradition for transformation and never passed on the chance to engage with anyone who sought Him or begged for healing.

And rather than view His behavior as admirable or kind, the customs and socialites of His time labeled Jesus' behavior as "shocking" and "inappropriate." Are you acquainted with the sting of a label, too? The stigma of being anything other than "enough." Well, Jesus certainly created a stir in His lifetime! In fact, the only thing more astonishing than His actions were the results of His actions!

Yet, because Jesus was a man steeped in custom, one could easily mistake His behavior for indifference. The thing is, Jesus was born of Jewish nationality, and the Jews could trace their lineage back to the Israelite people of the Old Testament. The Israelites became known as the Jewish people only after they were displaced from their homeland and scattered among other nations. Yet, despite their dispersion, devout Jews continued to live by the same standards that God had given to their ancestors. These standards, held as their law, dictated how they should eat, speak, and behave and signaled vast differences between the Jews and the world around them. For instance, instead of following numerous gods as the neighboring nations did, God required the Jews to worship Him only. Through their unique way of living, the Jews sought to draw a watching world to the knowledge of a unique God.

But over time, the Pharisees, an elite group of Jewish religious scholars, began to encourage obligations beyond God's original requests. And by Jesus' time, the Jewish law swelled from an abundance of restrictions and rules. And more rules. And a few more rules. And did I mention rules? Without even noticing, the Pharisees made things more about themselves than God, as we humans do best. Rather than bring glory to God, these additional rules simply brought praise to the Pharisees and fueled their pride, for the Pharisees were not content with being good—they wanted to be the best. And though their heightened levels to the law only succeeded in adding a suffocating list to an already unobtainable bar, the Pharisees really did try to measure up! And their relentless efforts managed to convince most people that the Pharisees could scale the bar of perfection.

Imagining these esteemed, highly decorated guys, you can almost hear Jesus gush, "These are my people!" But before you envision fist pumps or chest bumps, prepare to be amazed. You might even laugh out loud! For Jesus left no room for imagination in the following passage:

> "Woe to you, teachers of the law and Pharisees, you hypocrites! You give a tenth of your spices—mint, dill and cumin. But you have neglected the more important matters of the law—justice, mercy and faithfulness. You should have practiced the latter, without neglecting the former. You blind guides! You strain out a gnat but swallow a camel. "Woe to you, teachers of the law and Pharisees, you hypocrites! You clean the outside of the cup and dish, but inside they are full of greed and self-indulgence. Blind Pharisee! First clean the inside of the cup and dish, and then the outside also will be clean. "Woe to you, teachers of the law and Pharisees, you hypocrites! You are like

whitewashed tombs, which look beautiful on the outside but on the inside are full of the bones of the dead and everything unclean. In the same way, on the outside you appear to people as righteous but on the inside you are full of hypocrisy and wickedness. "You snakes! You brood of vipers! How will you escape being condemned to hell?"

Matthew 23:23-28, 33

Yow. Hypocrites? Snakes? Why did the Pharisees' hard work and credentials leave Jesus unimpressed? Because Jesus has always been interested in more than a show. More than a façade. More than elbow grease.

Jesus zeroes in on the heart.

So, no, Jesus didn't turn His nose up at the little kids who bounded around His feet, despite their low status in society. Nor did Jesus consider it a waste of time to talk to a woman—even a woman who had accumulated four failed marriages and a current live-in boyfriend. He would not brush aside a criminal or a thief who came to Him with questions, and He never ran from the dead or the sick as His culture would have dictated.

For within those lengthy rules of the Jewish law, strict regulations mandated steps for dealing with disease or handling the dead, whether animals or people. Contact with death or sickness classified a person as "unclean" or "defiled" for days. Even a woman's monthly cycle would qualify her as unclean and untouchable. For an unclean person to be "clean" again, they needed to complete lengthy purification procedures, and harsh punishment occurred if anyone did not maintain these strict rules of cleanliness. No doubt, Jesus knew these significant rules well and held to them most of the time, understanding that these rules protected the community from spreading disease in those days.

But anytime the letter of the law obstructed an opportunity to show kindness or love, Jesus astounded others with His preference. So while touching a diseased, contagious leper would have jeopardized others, Jesus gave no second thought to touching a leper and healing him. When a woman suffering from a bleeding disorder touched the hem of Jesus' garment, He turned to face her instead of screaming and running away—fast.

For Jesus zeroes in on the heart.

LOOKING PAST APPEARANCES

But our hearts represent a trip hazard for us. Because of their hidden anatomy, we insist that the proper tactics keep our innermost thoughts hidden. So we channel all our attention: We toss up smoke and mirrors for a superficial show and never stop scanning to gauge our show's effectiveness. But it's ironic when the tricks we employ to fool others manage to deceive us as well! Entrapped by the sole concern of keeping up appearances, we play our part, heedless that no amount of flashy productions, Oscar-worthy performances, or deep polishing can keep the rust and grime in the recesses of our hearts from seeping into the view of an all-seeing God. We become so consumed with looking outward that we neglect to look inward and see the heart lying right before our eyes. Inevitably, we will trip over that heart and faceplant into our own props. But all along, our hearts have laid fully exposed to God because the ploys that distract us and others do not faze Him. He fans away the smoke and looks past the mirrors—to zero in on the heart.

While our condition may sound hopeless, good news lies on the flip side. When I say nothing can distract God, blind His vision, or play tricks on His eyes, our instinct is to focus on the worst prospect: Our acts will not fool Him as they fool the people around us. And, of course, we wish for Him to see us as the world does.

Ah, but now the beauty is starting to break through. What impresses the world does *not* impress God. The looks, the accolades, the bank accounts, the possessions, the social media likes, and the followers are all shuffled out of the way. Yes, God sees us as no one else can. And though our hearts lay fully revealed to Him, our hearts lay fully *equal* before Him, too. Because when He removes all the worldly fluff, nothing remains to rank one's heart as better or worse than another's. What a beautiful thing that no temporary, earthly status will ever alter a person's worth in God's eyes.

Jesus always looked past appearances. Once, while Jesus observed several wealthy individuals presenting large monetary gifts for temple offerings, He commended a widow who had contributed a single penny instead. Surpassing dollars and cents, Jesus calculated that the wealthy individuals gave from their abundance, while the widow gave all she had. To Jesus, the widow's devotion was priceless. Another time, when Jesus found an angry crowd picking up stones to kill a woman caught in adultery, He did not choose to side with the law. Rather, with *one sentence,* He disarmed all her accusers. His powerful words? Jesus said, "Let any one of you who is without sin be the first to throw a stone at her" (John 8:7b). With that, Jesus silenced the accusers in mid shout. After several moments of silence, the accusers slowly picked up their jaws, closed their mouths, softened their furrowed brows, set down their stones, and, one by one, walked away.

Praise God. He is still the God who sees.

Praise God. He can still silence all your accusers and critics.

Because He is still more intent on redeeming your future than undoing your past.

Praise God. He is still the God who comes near.

He is still the God more interested in your heart than your outward appearance.

He continues to be the God who repeatedly loves on the unlovable, those not held in esteem by any worldly standard.

He is immune to the threats posed by any human condition or situation.

He remains the only one who can walk into the mess of sin and walk out undefiled.

He can still shift the "unclean" to "clean."

And He is still unafraid to enter any life story—especially yours.

For He knows who ultimately holds the paintbrush on the canvas of your life.

And there is nothing—nothing, nothing—that He cannot redeem, heal, resurrect, transform, or restore to totally brand-new.

Even if you don't have a thing of value in the rearview mirror, more than restoring previous things, God can also introduce brand spanking new things that you never possessed in the first place—things that are a cut above what was absent, lacking, defective, or just plain screwed up.

So please reread that last list as many times as needed! Highlight, earmark, or rip out the page and hang it up. Do whatever it takes to cement those words into your heart and mind.

CALLING THE SICK

Though we can say that Jesus will never snub us for our past or present circumstances, it's hard not to imagine our experiences collecting in an ever-growing pile. One after another, we add to our pile until we are sure our experiences form a wall that keeps Jesus from reaching or seeing us. Worst of all, we fear the dirtiness stuffed within our wall keeps Jesus from even caring to consider us. But, spoiler alert: Whether your wall presents as high or low, freshly stacked or old and rotten, it will not intimidate Jesus. He isn't waiting for your wall of circumstances to crumble, just the wall around your heart. All you have to do is admit, "Yes, I have jumbled my life with disorder and difficult circumstances, but I believe You can help me sort through the chaos."

If you are still doubtful that Jesus could be interested in your life, then find assurance in Jesus' words, "It is not the healthy who need a doctor, but the sick. I have not come to call the righteous, but sinners" (Mark 2:17).

Do you see it now? *Your experiences and sin cannot keep you from God—only your heart can. Your heart alone holds the opportunity to accept or walk away from God's offer.*

Jesus was never dumbstruck by anyone's past. He knew our lives would include mistakes and regrets. *He would not have chosen to die for us if no reason existed for Him to do so! What a lie the enemy has sold you if you believe you are not "good enough" or "ready enough" to come to Jesus just as you are right now!* Why, Jesus promises rejoicing in heaven over *every* sinful person who comes to God! Let that sink in: All of heaven joins in celebration for *one sinner*—instead of any amount of "righteous" people who find their own efforts sufficient and, as a result, see no need for God. Jesus came for sinners, the ones afflicted with the sickness of sin. Yes, He celebrates those who have already received the remedy for their sins. But His search, His driving purpose, is still to reach those who need Him most—those who think a cure is nonexistent or beyond their reach.

So while thankfulness overtakes me that we have started this necessary conversation, and relief floods me for any insight you have found because of it, the conversation cannot stop here. Even if you acquire all the knowledge in the world, unless you choose to *use* that knowledge, the possession alone amounts to nothing. Only when truth translates into action will it produce any impact on your heart or life. We cannot say one thing but proceed to do the opposite. If we can admit that changes should occur, we will want to be willing and bold enough to make those changes. We can no longer deny the enemy haunting us, the sin camping in our souls, the secret shadows blanketing our hearts, or the despair refusing to depart through our strength alone.

So if you have never surrendered your life and allowed Jesus to be your Savior, would you consider praying a simple prayer right now? Either a prayer in your own words or the prayer that follows? No prescribed words, scripts, or guidelines exist. You only need to bring a humble heart needing a healing touch. So if you are willing, please pray:

"Today, Jesus, I come to you with my life exposed and my heart surrendered. I no longer want to run from You because I realize You already know all about me. But even though You know about my sin and all my circumstances, You still love me. I admit that I cannot save myself or control my life. So I ask you, Jesus, to enter my life and my heart today. Please bring Your healing and restoration into my life. Make me new from the inside out. Thank you, Jesus, for loving me before I even knew You and for patiently waiting on me to come to You. Amen."

My sweet friends, your yesterdays cannot haunt you anymore, and your sin can never define you ever again.

For you no longer face an accuser.

And do you hear it? That's heaven rejoicing right now—because of you!

Whether you just became a follower of Jesus or have had a relationship with Him for a long time, never let the enemy delude you into believing that any sin could somehow ruin your life. And stay strong as you continue to experience healing and growth amid shortcomings and setbacks because you will and *should* continue to grow in your Christian walk. Absolutely *no* shame exists in continuing to need God's grace daily, for we will never be completely free from sin on this side of heaven. Yet, we *can and will* be free from the chains of sin, the control of sin, and the sentence of sin—when the God who sees us enters the scene!

"The thief comes only to steal and kill and destroy; I have come that they may have life, and have it to the full" (John 10:10).

Do not give up on yourself.

Give up on sin.

Quit doing life without God.

Eyes up.

Game on.

Yep, shame no longer has any place here.

The enemy's previous tricks? They no longer work here.

The enemy's game? We're quitting it and calling his bluff.

8

SPREADING IT

How much of our lives do we spend in anticipation and preparation for future intentions? Getting ready for the day. Studying for the exam. Planning the trip. Waiting to reach a certain age. Hoping for a response. Learning the job. The list of things that vie for our attention is never-ending, and doubtless, we invest vast amounts of time and energy in pursuit of things that are all bound to vanish.

Perhaps you have never been assigned the challenge—I mean "honor"—of coordinating a Thanksgiving meal. But let me tell you, Thanksgiving naps are a staple of the holiday menu for reasons that exceed the tryptophan levels in turkey! In all sincerity, I do enjoy cooking for my family and friends, but home-cooked meals do not just happen—and needless to say, Thanksgiving does *not* just happen. I must assemble a full-scale culinary attack to pull off that one monumental meal. The first phase requires a day to plan the menu and several hours to shop for groceries. The second phase commences with a kitchen battle and is executed through 10-plus hour shifts over two to three days as I prep side dishes, vegetables, desserts, and the main course.

But despite my best-laid plans, experience haunts me. It reminds me that a formidable foe will manage to add itself to the guest list, pull up a chair, and stick a fork in my dreams. Once again, I will face off with this undesirable guest: Irony. I might need ample time to complete my mission, but not Irony. Nope, its visit will last about as long as dessert on my plate—to be blunt, that's not long! The odds aren't fair: The meal doesn't stand a chance when pitted against agile, hungry participants. Within mere minutes, the meal succumbs, and only a wake of crumbs remains, thanks to Irony—and no thanks to my own fork!

Indifferent to the time I spend strategizing and amassing a food arsenal, the curtain will close on my culinary display almost as soon as it opens. My investment will never equate with my return on the meal. Yes, as the holiday prompts me, I am thankful for every laugh, story, and full belly surrounding the table. And when counting my blessings, I won't overlook the fact that people are willing to eat my food without the use of force! But while the experience can fill me physically, it cannot fill me completely. Aside from the food I consume, a part of me will still crave *more*—a more substantial satisfaction. Although, if a meal could last, say, as long as vegetables on a child's plate, I'm convinced I would have an easier time feeling satisfied! Because, in my opinion, *that* sounds like an extended ending worth savoring!

HUMANITY'S UNIQUENESS

Yet the only thing better than a good ending is a good thing that never ends. So why do we chase after an elusive reward or pin all our hopes on something guaranteed to end? Wouldn't it be more advantageous to channel our efforts into something that will not end? According to my calculations, one possible subject will never end: people. Confirming this hunch, John 11:25-26 tells us, "Jesus said to her, 'I am the resurrection and the life. The one who believes in Me will live, even though they die; and whoever lives by believing in Me will never die. Do you believe this?'"

If you, too, believe that there is more to life than our current existence and that human souls are eternal, what better investment could exist than contributing to someone's soul? What other yield could possibly rival eternity? Even if the academic degree opens the door you had hoped for, the trip exceeds the reviews, or the Thanksgiving meal rivals a five-star restaurant—an end looms. At some point, hunger will devour the meal. The trip will reach the end of the line. The career will clock out. New insight may eclipse the premier knowledge of today. The asset could depreciate or be exhausted. You name it: Everything we do and know on this earth will end. Everything—except the people.

Since the Creation story, we see the uniqueness of humanity apart from the rest of the created world. Our humans souls differentiate us from the natural world, and God created our souls with eternity in mind. Out of all creation, God made humans alone, in His image, by uniquely embedding each person with distinct facets of His nature. One person may reflect God's creativity, another His attention to detail, and yet another His empathy. But He has stamped each person with intentional and undeniable value. Despite infinite combinations, each person is an exclusive, living expression of God.

So when sin threatens to mar these expressions and remove our God-given identities, God moves to restore us with an accurate understanding of our worth. And when Satan attempts to fracture our souls by diverting our eternal aim, God intervenes to retrieve and redirect every wandering soul.

The Bible brims over with accounts of God's attempts to win back people's hearts. God's mercy and patience saturate each story. He refuses no one but waits with His arms wide open in anticipation of our return. Yet, as the Bible characters encountered, our human nature always draws us away from those arms. Our arrogance begs us to cling to our own strength, and our fear urges us to stick to the familiar ruts in our lives.

THE PROPHET HOSEA

God knows His ways seem counterintuitive to us. Far from commonplace, we could never anticipate the mindset behind God's character because He exceeds anything we could ever imagine. So, knowing our limitations, God will often teach us by using relatable analogies to stir up visual images that we can wrap our minds around.

Throughout history, God asked specific individuals whom He called prophets to be messengers of these lessons to His people. And the prophets usually shared one thing in common—it's safe to say that the crowd did not vote them most popular. In the best-case scenario, the people received the prophets' messages as radical concepts. But more often than not, the people took the messages as direct insults, for the messages sometimes called them out for their behavior, challenged them toward change, or nudged them to return to God. But, as with us, the people weren't fond of change and experienced more discomfort than warm fuzzies after hearing the truth. So the people often ignored, teased or persecuted the prophets.

Following suit, God assigned the prophet Hosea a problematic task of no laughing matter either—a request he never saw coming! You see, Hosea was a prophet to the northern kingdom of Israel right before its eventual fall in 722 BC. You could say that God sent him as a last-ditch effort to persuade Israel to rebuild their relationship with Him before their actions reaped dreadful consequences that would snowball through the pages of history.

God told Hosea to "marry a promiscuous woman and have children with her" (Hosea 1:2). Yes, you read that right. Hosea entered a marriage with a woman who either had a promiscuous history or would develop a promiscuous inclination during their marriage. Many of us fear marriage's unknowns, but Hosea knew *exactly* what to fear. Why in the world would God make this strange request of Hosea?

The request was made for the Israelites' benefit and even ours today because God planned to use Hosea's marriage as a visual image of Israel's relationship with Him. Although the Israelites were everyday people, neither particularly admirable nor worthy of God's selection, God still chose them to be in a special relationship with Him. To maintain an accurate portrayal, God selected Hosea's future wife, Gomer, because she, too, lacked any desirable credentials. Gomer would play her role well and mirrored Israel's habitual chase for earthly pleasures over a relationship with God. Repeatedly, Gomer grew listless in her marriage and chose the fleeting over the forever. By doing so, she broke Hosea's heart. Oodles of times. Just as God's people had also broken His heart oodles of times.

So did I mention that God's ways can confound us? Because what would you tell poor Hosea to do faced with Gomer's behaviors and patterns? Leave her? Kick her to the curb? Run, buddy, run? Well, it would be natural for Gomer's behavior to elicit those responses. But if we remember, God had given Hosea an assignment, and Hosea had determined to follow that assignment to the letter. Opposite our instincts, God asked Hosea to treat Gomer as she did *not* deserve. On the contrary, He directed, "Go, show your love to your wife again, though she is loved by another man and is an adulteress. Love her as the Lord loves the Israelites" (Hosea 3:1). And without noted hesitation or delay, the very next verse tells us Hosea's reaction. "So I bought her for *fifteen shekels of silver* and about a homer and a lethek of barley" (Hosea 3:2, emphasis mine).

Though Hosea's obedience may have startled you, an unexpected word might have also caught your attention: bought. Hosea bought Gomer. For centuries, humans have participated in the tragedy of human trafficking, and the slave trade transpired in Biblical times as well. As the verse implies, Gomer's carefree living had resulted in some dire circumstances. Though once free, Gomer nose-dived into enslavement until, in all likelihood, she landed on a platform.

Naked and for sale. Stripped of all self-worth. Humiliated. Exposed. At rock bottom. According to Exodus 21:32, the price of an enslaved person during Biblical times was about thirty shekels.[12] Judging by her selling price, Gomer's value was only half of the going rate.

I would imagine she hung her head as bidders appraised her worth.

And I also imagine she doubted her ears as they discerned a familiar voice bidding for her.

A voice from her past.

Her estranged husband.

Yet, why would he be here?

And why would he ever bid on her?

Amid her disbelief, Hosea delivered Gomer the surprise of her life as he stepped forward, took her by the arm, covered her, and led her home.

Shocking love.

Yet, God's love always is.

Undeserved.

But that's the essence of mercy.

Imagining that startling exchange and the following days, we empathize with Hosea. How would it feel to look into the eyes of your betrayer every day? Could Hosea forget his marriage's sketchy past? How could Hosea love when he had no guarantee of his love's return but, in fact, had every reason to assume that it would not be?

On the flip side, we can empathize with Gomer as well. In disgrace, she returned, but could she forgive herself? Could she change? Would she allow herself to experience this unimaginable love?

Yet, we can't begin to imagine God's feelings, for the story of Hosea and Gomer expands beyond its representation of God's relationship with Israel to provide an analogy for the history of God's love story with humanity. While God longs for a relationship,

His affections fall on people more prone to leave than stay. He is in love with a people who cannot remain faithful. Yet God has gone to great lengths to redeem us, to purchase us back from our shame, and to give us another chance. Rather than leave us on the platforms of our past, He comes to us. Not because we earned His affection or gave a worthy performance. Not because He is only vaguely familiar with our history or is short a few details. No, even with full awareness, He still ventures to get up close and personal with us and all our past and present circumstances.

Just as Hosea went to Gomer in her worst moment, God also comes to us. He finds us, like Gomer, standing in a messy place, disgraced and alone, believing we have sunk too far, thinking we have no more options, and feeling convinced that the consequences are too hefty to face.

But beneath the dirt and grime, it still exists, unhidden from the Creator's eye—the living expression of God's image still bearing its stamp on *every* person. Value, though unhidden to the Creator's eye, may appear hidden from our eyes when buried beneath dirt and grime. The possibility of this oversight provides the necessity for this chapter: *There are living expressions of God's image who are living without the knowledge of their value.* Right now, their loneliness, vulnerability, or hopelessness overshadows their value. Because I have walked miles in those shoes, I do not wish to see anyone else head down that same relentless road.

CHANGING THE TIDE

So I have given up trying to hide my mess, for what good can a buried mess possibly produce? What benefit comes from leaving junk to rot away in the dark shadows of my soul? In my experience, rotting messes only grow funkier and refuse to stay hidden. No effort would be enough to mask my mess, delude others from its presence, or keep its stench from seeping out sooner or later—to my nose if no one else's.

No, I would prefer to take my mess, exchange its rancid per-
fumes, and invest in the eternal—in the living expressions of God
who are still bound, but are also bound for eternity.

Hiding my mistakes and misguided thoughts produces zero advantages for myself or others, so I find no better motivation to implement an alternate strategy: Stop cowering and toss off the blanket of regret smothering me. Perhaps, by exposing my mess to the world around me, even *one* girl or woman may see what led to my disaster, learn from my mistakes, disrupt the cycle—*and not repeat it*! Maybe you are the one person who needed to benefit from my mistakes, and if so, I could not be any more thankful or honored because you are *so* worth every step of my journey to reach you!

But I must admit: I still wonder, for there's a question that manages to both evade and challenge me as it withholds an answer. This gnawing question begs: Could there be *one more* person? Does anyone still need to hear the spiritual truths that introduce a fresh perspective? Would these insights enable her to spy potential, seize hope, claim joy, or step forward in a new mindset? If the answer is yes, then I am compelled to continue sharing my story by the deep desire that *one more* girl or woman can ditch her shame.

Forget her doubt.

Amputate her chains.

And turn her ship in a new direction.

If that happens, the tide will change—and as few people as possible will wind up as I did, as Gomer did.

Is it just me, or has "few" never sounded more colossal?

THE MESSIAH

If God didn't dumbfound us enough through Hosea's story, He's about to. His most shocking story in the Bible did not play out until almost seven hundred years after Hosea's time, but during those hundreds of years, the Israelites continued to look for the fulfillment of God's promises to them. His most tremendous promise pledged a future Messiah—a Savior to the people. But confusion arose when the Israelites tried to look for this eternal promise using their human eyesight. In so doing, they imagined a victorious earthly king who would overthrow all their enemies and oppressors. In short, they equated a savior with power.

Therefore, they never would have written the story the way God did. They would never have cast a helpless baby instead of a commanding warrior king. Nor would they have believed a poor carpenter's son could become a leader. But more than anything, *they never would have used the word "suffering" to describe their envisioned Messiah.*

Yet, this was the precise word that God chose for His description. He would send "a man of suffering, and familiar with pain" (Isaiah 53:3). Once again, we cannot predict God's ways. Even though the Israelites regarded political liberation as their ultimate desire, God's objective was grander than an insecure government, at best, and stretched beyond the threats of present enemies. God's target zeroed in on an eternal enemy—their sin.

A sacrifice was the only method to remedy their sin—a life for a life. God would not ignore this requirement—He would just fulfill it through an alternative approach. Instead of selecting an animal from a field, God chose a lamb substitute: His only Son, Jesus. And as a lamb, so did Jesus live—without fanfare or even a place to call home. The Israelites assumed that Jesus' humble lifestyle stemmed from his lack of pedigree, and finding zero indication of a promising political career, they found it easy to belittle or dismiss Him. Seeming to confirm their suspicions, Jesus did not ascend to a throne. Instead, He ascended a hill—to a cross—to face crucifixion, a fate reserved for the worst criminals in those days. But His life did not justify this treatment. Never once did Jesus sin, steal, cheat, or lie. Never once did He hurt or wound anyone. He did the reverse: Jesus healed others and lived a faultless, sinless life.

So why did He have to die?

He *didn't* have to—*He* didn't owe any debt.

But *we* did.

Our eternal enemy was holding us hostage and demanding payment in full on our account—but it was a debt that would bankrupt us.

The likelihood of repaying even a tiny portion of our debt was slim to none.

Because animal sacrifices provided only temporary appeasement for the law, the Israelites had to offer them day in and day out in a never-ending cycle. But Jesus' sinless life embodied a sacrifice so perfect and complete that it was necessary only once. His death checked all the law's boxes and shredded the bill tallying the accumulation of sin from all time.

Though He didn't have to die, Jesus chose to relinquish His life to save ours.

In a most lopsided trade, we handed Him our sin, and He deposited His righteousness into our account.

Could the Israelites make sense of it?

No.

Will we ever make sense of it?

No.

Because, again, the gracious, shocking love of God is not sensible.

We never would have written the Messiah's story as it played out, and I am guessing that most of us would have also scripted a different story for our lives. Without hesitation, if I could edit my life story into a DVD menu, I would navigate straight to my scenes of weakness or defeat, pluck them out of the lineup, and banish them to my deleted scenes. It's safe to presume that we would find no shortage of preferences to suffering if given the choice between suffering and any other alternative. Conflict and tension may serve well in a fiction plot, but our non-fiction lives prefer a more direct, uncluttered, uncontended path to triumph and success. Please and thank you. Yes, any logical person begs for redemption minus suffering and *definitely* minus any form of cross-bearing!

THE SKEPTICS

Well, Jesus' skeptics were logical too, and after the cross, they puffed out their chests: No way could this man have been the Messiah. Why, the proposed King lay dead, exposed as an *obvious* imposter. So in arrogant confidence, Jesus' haters reveled in triumph, and Rome claimed victory.

At least for a little while.

Until one early morning, two days later, the ground and graves shook, and the giant rock sealing Jesus' tomb rolled to make way for a miracle! The stage was set, and the resurrected Jesus stretched, folded His grave clothes, strolled out of His tomb, and refused to toss a single glance back. But disbelief ran rampant as Jesus began to reveal His risen state. Until one could see Jesus for himself, the hurdle of doubt was, sometimes, unscalable.

As it happened, one of the greatest skeptics called himself one of Jesus' closest friends. Thomas, one of Jesus' twelve disciples, had spent the last several years learning and following Jesus' ministry. But like many of us, Thomas didn't see how suffering could fit into his understanding of the Messiah. Thomas staunchly proclaimed, "Unless I see the nail marks in His hands and put my finger where the nails were, and put my hand into His side, I will not believe" (John 20:25).

Unless Thomas could see the physical imprints of the crucifixion on Jesus' body, he would not believe it. He could not ignore the improbability of such a rare phenomenon as resurrection—especially when he studied the facts of Jesus' death. Soldiers had driven nails through Jesus' hands and feet, hoisted His cross to a crowd's witness, monitored His slow suffocation, and pierced His side to confirm His death. No, no! Thomas would not go there! Gambling with logic is where he drew the line. It was just too high of a risk for disappointment.

But in a gracious gift to Thomas, as much as to those of us who would experience doubt in the centuries to come, Jesus indulged him. "Put your finger here; see My hands. Reach out your hand and put it into My side. Stop doubting and believe" (John 20:27).

How's that for a curveball? Thomas' doubt came unglued, and he knew in an instant: This was Jesus. This *was* the Messiah.

SCARS

Did you catch what authenticated Jesus?

His scars did.

What authenticates any of us as survivors?

Our scars do as well.

Some of us were former softball stars. The scars on our legs recall our victory slides into home plate.

Some of us were former superheroes. Or not so much. The scar on our elbow suggests we found that one out the hard way.

However, perhaps our other scars are even more telling—not any other surface scars courtesy of a victorious or humorous adventure but the scars beneath our skin courtesy of wounds to our soul. Unlike surface scars, internal scars do not promise to harden nor pave the way for healing, but without fail, they form to veil the tender areas lying beneath them. Our body works on autopilot to enshroud any tender spot before being exploited as a potential trigger—or worse, a personal kryptonite. Lurking even behind our consciousness sometimes, these invisible scars don't call attention to their presence. We will never be able to point to them, yet we carry them daily because these scars are branded on our hearts and seared in our minds.

And as much as we may resent the scars beneath our surface, they provide our proof: We are no strangers to suffering. Yet, if we are tempted to count them as a weakness, we will miss the potential packed within them and rob them of their ability to reassure others, "Yeah, I get it. I, too, have walked hand in hand with suffering."

Sure, by feeling Jesus' breath, one could have quickly confirmed that Jesus was alive. And by observing Him walk, talk, and eat among them, many witnesses were convinced that Jesus did, indeed, conquer death. But in the presence of such power—power that left behind an empty grave and embarrassed the shame of the cross—would they have made a *personal* connection with Jesus? If Jesus had taken a poll to see who else had hung on a cross and lived to tell the tale, it would have been a quick poll! Safe to say, no one could have concurred, "That's my story!" Instead, those polled would have replied with blank stares and the sound of crickets.

It is far more likely that this stark division would have carved a Grand Canyon between Jesus and those around Him rather than tailored an invitation to draw near. It's just not our tendency to equate prestige with humility, elevation with accessibility, or power with sensitivity. So while Jesus' power qualified Him as the Messiah, it did not automatically qualify Him as approachable or understanding. And though He was technically near, our ability to relate with Him was still a long way off.

Though hindsight is always 20/20, you have no idea what the outcome will be while in the midst of a situation. Your view is too narrow. However, after you know the outcome, it becomes easier to see how all the smaller events fit together to form a bigger picture. But standing at the foot of the bloody cross, we would not have had clear vision. Only now, with the whole story before us in the Bible, can we have any 20/20 insight. Yet the crucifixion served up sorrow for those who witnessed it up close. However, from God's perspective, the crucifixion delivered joy. Up close, the crucifixion singled out the worst day ever. From God's viewpoint, it marked the world's best day ever. Up close, it appeared that evil had won. But from God's vantage point, He saw that justice had triumphed.

What seemed like the worst day ever, the greatest injustice in all history, and the most devastating thing to ever happen—was not an accident.

Nor was it a surprise.

It was a *plan*.

And God's plan operated in light of eternity.

Since the beginning of time, He commanded a plan to save people from a sinful debt they could never repay or work off themselves.

Jesus' death satisfied the punishment due us and canceled our debt.

His resurrection overpowered the enemy's chokehold.

Eternity's door opened and presented an unmerited welcome to us.

Mercy triumphed over sin—and mercy still does.

Yet we can only appreciate any of that because of our larger perspective. If our view was limited to the crucifixion, we could not distinguish any good at work. And those who witnessed the crucifixion would have never caught it either—without the help of the scars, that is.

Jesus' scars provided Him no personal benefit. He needed no assurance of what He had endured during the crucifixion. Beyond that, if Jesus could heal disabilities, cleanse lepers, cast out demons, and rise from the dead to defeat death for eternity—is it logical to believe that scars posed an issue for Him? Since God restored Jesus' body from every one of death's effects, we can be certain: He could have wiped away any scars as well.

Yet Jesus' scars were not an oversight.

He may have left His grave clothes and the tomb behind Him, but He chose to carry out His scars.

Why?

Beyond authenticating Himself as an all-powerful Savior, His scars did what power could not: They bridged the gap between His triumph and our suffering. His scars qualified Him as approachable and able to relate to our suffering. And Jesus kept them so we could dare to believe that suffering sometimes paves the road to victory.

Jesus' scars do not communicate embarrassment or indicate defeat.

On the contrary, Jesus' scars advertise hope!

Rather than deny or dodge facts, scars confirm: Yes, there's a story here that involved injury and pain, but that pain wasn't the end of the story. The fact that a scar exists versus a gaping, bloody wound indicates a measure of healing. When we can witness the closure of a once raw wound, detect the collapse of a once oppressive injury, and note the improvement in a once debilitating circumstance, we, like Thomas, collect evidence that builds a case for hope. As the evidence compiles, we find confidence to believe that one day we, too, can change and feel stronger than before. Hope hands down the verdict: We, too, can replace injury with strength.

Yes, Jesus *chose* to keep His scars.

So they could tell a story to those who need to see before they can believe.

So why do you and I bear scars?

For the exact same reason.

What registers as a bad thing at first glance can actually reveal something good when given a second glance. To be sure, a horrific, cruel act caused Jesus' scars, but His scars defied their infliction by producing good when used to tell a story of healing and hope to the world. And my sweet friends, your scars are no different.

For your scars can supply assurance to others too.

Oh, they may look unlike anyone else's scars, but they exist to tell a specific story of survival, healing, and hope. Even if your scars lie beyond the sphere of natural sight, they possess the means to surface.

Through your words, your scars can throw out a hint.

And through your actions, your scars can throw up a flare.

But it's through your story that your scars can throw out a lifeline.

We live in a world *packed* with wounded hearts needing a tourniquet of hope.

Authentic hope that quiets the rush of doubt.

Stops the damage from seeping out.

And summons the strength to believe that healing is not only possible but it is also within reach.

Your scars form the answer for those who are reaching and searching for visible, tangible evidences of hope.

Through Christ's scars, hope arrived for the world.

Through your scars, hope can arrive in your corner of the world—or anywhere.

Hope's boundary corresponds to how wide you spread your healing, the lengths you run to pass along your joy, and the depths you allow your story to trickle down to soothe the next bleeding soul.

It all comes down to this question: What will you let pass through your scars?

GRAVE STATISTICS

Thomas asked what we all ask in the thick of life's pain and despair: "How?" And friends, others will want to ask you the same question: How did you pull through?

For if you were not aware before, I hope you now know— you are not an anomaly. Statistics verify that a grave number of gals can relate to an equally grave number of devastating sexual experiences such as ours. These statistics are not faceless, though. We know them as friends, sisters, cousins, in-laws, neighbors, co-workers, teammates, roommates, or acquaintances. Whatever title they wear, we know some are hiding in the corners, masking their shame, denying the cost, yet crying themselves to sleep in the ashes of sexual brokenness, despair, and disappointment. We know because we used to live the same way before grace arrived on the scene, and mercy offered a new start.

How can we leave them there? Alone in the battle for their life?

I hope your answer matches mine: I simply cannot. My rescue celebration isn't as sweet if I neglect to recognize those not celebrating yet. And it's hard to charge forward in good conscience if I refuse to look back when I feel a tug from those still grasping for a helping hand.

My prayer is that you have now found the hope, love, worth, peace, and joy you have been seeking—and that you found all these things solely in Jesus' extended, scarred hands. I also pray this journey has assured you that nothing lies beyond God's miraculous power to transform or resurrect. Instead of reaching a plateau, may your healing only increase as you submit your scars to the fellow souls you encounter along your way. And together, may you both rejoice as you "bestow on them a crown of beauty instead of ashes, the oil of joy instead of mourning, and a garment of praise instead of a spirit of despair" (Isaiah 61:3).

REWRITES

You have a story. I have a story. While the specifics of our stories may differ, our unique details are the perfect tools for unlocking a unique story in someone else. We cannot go back in time. We cannot erase the facts of our stories. We cannot deny the experiences that have brought us to the present. But now, even though the facts of our stories are not changing, *we* are. And though we can spot differences in our stories, we are more impressed by the staggering resemblances we have discovered—similarities that unite us with stories spanning the pages of history and thousands of years! The stories of Rahab, Hagar, Gomer, or any other woman who ever approached Jesus without her society's stamp of approval could just as well be our story today. The names, places, and timelines vary, but again, we race past the differences because we are captivated by the beautiful common denominator central to each encounter: the heart of Jesus. Jesus never changes the facts of these women's stories, but He certainly never leaves the women unchanged, either. He comes face to face with their situations but has no issues deciphering their mess from their identity or untangling their imposed shame from their innate worth.

He does not dawdle in the chapters already written in these women's lives but flips to the blank, upcoming chapters to edit them with a heavenly twist—a new ending. The world insisted these women had no options and their endings were inevitable. But Jesus didn't get that memo, so He initiated a rewrite in their lives. Life endings, previously foreshadowed as hopeless, now read: Whole. Restored. Cleansed. Pure. Renewed. Valuable. Rescued. Significant. Redeemed.

If we hadn't experienced some of those rewrites ourselves, it would all sound too good to be true. But here we are, familiar with the view from the wrong side of purity, holding what we thought were all the wrong pieces for a "good" story, and yet, confident that our purely wrong stories now read as a tribute to pure grace.

As it turned out, the wrong side of purity ushered us into the right side for mercy—the only side where a Savior waited with a purely wrong solution: pure, unmerited love.

It *is* an unparalleled, ridiculous love, and many can't get past the glaring absurdity of a love that strikes them as so illogical and wrong to dispense.

But, hey, we are used to "wrong" being a part of our story. We'll just have to get used to the idea that "wrong" will no longer hold the lead part.

For it is grace's turn at center stage. And even though it sounds like a fluffy word, we know that there's nothing wimpy or flimsy about it. This grace can block any attempt to throw shade and prevent any shame from sticking because it has already taken on the cross—and won.

So any intimidation or taunts of the cross now gag under a pile of wrongs and injustices stamped "paid in full." And what once was a barricaded tomb now lies unobstructed to confirm: Nothing and no one can keep you here. You are free. The tomb is not your home. So leave your experience in the grave because life is waiting.

Maneuvering out of the tomb, you shouldn't be surprised when your hand brushes against a tender reminder—a folded pile of grave clothes with an envelope lying on top. The envelope bears your name. Considering that only one person has ever left His grave clothes behind, it is no wonder Who wrote you the letter that reads,

I love you. Just as you are. Whatever is weighing you down, please don't waste any energy trying to fix it, tidy it, or sneak it by. Just bring it to Me and lay it down. You've been carrying it too long—let Me take the load.

Take a deep breath in, then let it go. Hush your mind, and let your heart settle. I know you are afraid, and I know you are hurting. Even though you couldn't see Me then, in that place, in those moments, I saw it all, and My heart ached as I collected your tears. I was closer than you believed, for I am never nearer to you than when you feel utterly crushed—when life plunges you into its lowest valley, and your desperation rises to its highest peak. I give you My promise: No matter the time or place, I will always come to your rescue when you call. Nothing can stop Me. Even in ways beyond your comprehension, I fight for you—daily—using every means at My disposal to defend and surround you because you are My most valuable treasure.

I make no accidents or mistakes—especially when it comes to you because you are My pride and joy. I smiled when I colored your eyes and tuned your laugh. I hand-picked every detail about you and then counted down the days until you were born, longing for the day when you would know Me, too—not through shallow facts or secondary sources but through personal experience. Everything I've done is so you could know My heart and call Me a friend. If you accept My friendship, someday we will sit together and gather the puzzle pieces of your life, and you'll connect them one by one. You will trace My handiwork in every piece down to the smallest detail. At times, I've drawn lines and told the enemy, "No farther." Other times, I have sculpted or expanded your bounds. Yet all of it will seamlessly assemble into an exquisite bigger picture—showcasing My ability to bring wholeness from what poses as holes, mismatches, or loose strings in your life. I won't waste a single piece because I'm a master of making beauty and finding purpose.

My goodness is unimaginable, for I'm like nothing you've ever known or experienced! Though the world has given you far more reasons to fear than to trust, your heart could never be safer than with Me. Every question you raise, I can answer. Every fear that haunts you, I can unmask. And every vacancy consuming you, I can occupy. I won't hurt you, abandon you, or disappoint you, and no one can snatch you from My hands or derail My plans for your life.

I'm working on something big. It's a global story, and I've included a part for you—in fact, you are the only one who can fill the specific qualifications. Though it seems purely wrong or impossible, I will fuse all the elements of your story into an ending that defies any expectations and is nothing short of purely beautiful. There is so much more ahead of you! You have no reason to look back except to pitch the dead weight of your washed-up shame into the convenient, empty tomb behind you. Before you pass by this moment, take it in. Nothing is holding you back, for I have placed you on the right side of purity because I've never seen you through the lens of your story. Yes, your story has elements of brokenness, pain, harm, and regret. But, you? You're not dirty, ruined, invisible, or a disappointment, regardless of the places you've been or the situations you've encountered. The enemy doesn't want you to do the math, but the numbers don't lie: The greater the mess you hand Me, the greater the miracles I can hand back. So lift your head with assurance and confidence—you are more than just your body.

I assigned no date to this letter because it is timeless: My mercy is as necessary today as it will be tomorrow or a thousand tomorrows from now. Although being good is a noble aim, no single story starts there or ever reaches that mark. So an imperfect story is a given rather than an exception. And if everyone's story is flawed, then you stand on level ground. But since your life has been paired with grace, the slate is clean. Grace ushers in the freedom that steamrolls comparison and striving—and I paid too high of a price for you not to live in this freedom.

On any scale and in every capacity, you never have to wonder if you are enough in My eyes because the answer is always a resounding "Yes!" Yes, you are enough to soak up My attention. Yes, you are enough to keep Me glued to the seat beside you. And yes, you are enough to captivate My heart for all eternity. But of supreme importance, I am enough: I am enough for whatever lies ahead and enough to restore whatever lies behind.

My defense goes before you, My authority is behind you, and My presence is beside you. Yet My glory? Well, My glory is within your story—to be more specific, it's in your story's broken, twisted, hopeless pieces. Because when situations shift, tables turn, or hope arises, and zero logical explanations can explain how or why, a spotlight shines directly on Me. Now I hope you see why your purely wrong story is purely perfect: Your pure worst rolls out the red carpet for My pure best to go to work. And how I love serving up a good shock and awe!

It's a big world that needs to be changed, and shame won't go down without a fight. But I'm offering you the chance to join Me and witness as I redefine "impossible" with "possible."

How's that for a curveball?

Has God demolished your doubt? Clobbered your shame?

Good. Then now is the time to believe and to live as if we do.

Admittedly, we will contend with sexual brokenness until the end of time, for this issue has existed in every social circle, in every corner of the world, and throughout every age. Yet it shouldn't be a secret: Mercy wins. So, although we face a daunting task, I am up for the challenge because I believe that a valiant Ally stands ready at our side.

How about you? Will you be content to keep this healing to yourself? Or are you ready to start spreading it?

Lord God,

You are the God of the impossible.

When Your enemies thought they could crucify You, You killed their plans.

Nails meant to anchor You to a cross inadvertently anchored our freedom.

And You still transform everything placed in Your hands.

So when we hand You our life, hurts heal.

Broken pieces converge.

Despair surrenders to hope.

Scars shape into stories.

Ashes scatter for joy.

And grace ousts shame.

Thank You for stamping each of our hearts with Your priceless image.

May You bless our every effort as we aspire to live in these truths and share them with the precious girls and women You place around us.

And may shame never cover our worth again or echo louder than Your glory in our lives!

Amen.

RESOURCES

At any time during your healing journey, if the process becomes too much, if you develop any concerning symptoms, or if you need safety, please seek professional help or support from an appropriate resource. Some national crisis organizations providing various assistance are listed below[13,14]:

The National Domestic Violence Hotline
1-800-799-7233 (SAFE)
www.ndvh.org

National Dating Abuse Helpline
1-866-331-9474
www.loveisrespect.org

National Child Abuse Hotline/Childhelp
1-800-4-A-CHILD (1-800-422-4453)
www.childhelp.org

National Suicide Prevention Lifeline
1-800-273-8255 (TALK)
www.suicidepreventionlifeline.org

National Human Trafficking Resource
Center/Polaris Project
Call: 1-888-373-7888
Text: HELP to BeFree (233733)
www.polarisproject.org

National Runaway Safeline
1-800-RUNAWAY or 1-800-786-2929
www.1800runaway.org

National Sexual Assault Hotline
1-800-656-4673 (HOPE)
www.rainn.org

Substance Abuse and Mental Health Services Administration
SAMHSA'S National Helpline
1-800-662-HELP (4357)
www.samhsa.gov

SCRIPTURE SNIPPETS

If you do not have access to a Bible, I want to provide you with a collection of verses until you can get your own Bible.

Even if you already have a Bible, these categorized verses could be a convenient reference tool or a springboard for a deeper search.

I grouped the verses to create encouraging collections for whenever you feel ashamed, doubtful, hopeless, fearful, or unloved.

ASHAMED? REMEMBER:

Psalm 51:16-17

Going through the motions doesn't please you, a flawless performance is nothing to you. I learned God-worship when my pride was shattered. Heart-shattered lives ready for love don't for a moment escape God's notice.

Psalm 65:2b–3

We all arrive at your doorstep sooner or later, loaded with guilt, Our sins too much for us—but you get rid of them once and for all.

Jeremiah 31:18-20

"I've heard the contrition of Ephraim. Yes, I've heard it clearly, saying, 'You trained me well. You broke me, a wild yearling horse, to the saddle. Now put me, trained and obedient, to use. You are my God. After those years of running loose, I repented. After you trained me to obedience, I was ashamed of my past, my wild, unruly past. Humiliated, I beat on my chest. Will I ever live this down?' "Oh! Ephraim is my dear, dear son, my child in whom I take pleasure! Every time I mention his name, my heart bursts with longing for him! Everything in me cries out for him. Softly and tenderly I wait for him." God's Decree.

Zechariah 10:6

"I'll put muscle in the people of Judah; I'll save the people of Joseph. I know their pain and will make them good as new. They'll get a fresh start, as if nothing had ever happened. And why? Because I am their very own God, I'll do what needs to be done for them.

John 3:17-18

God didn't go to all the trouble of sending his Son merely to point an accusing finger, telling the world how bad it was. He came to help, to put the world right again. Anyone who trusts in him is acquitted; anyone who refuses to trust him has long since been under the death sentence without knowing it. And why? Because of that person's failure to believe in the one-of-a-kind Son of God when introduced to him.

John 8:6b-11

Jesus bent down and wrote with his finger in the dirt. They kept at him, badgering him. He straightened up and said, "The sinless one among you, go first: Throw the stone." Bending down again, he wrote some more in the dirt. Hearing that, they walked away, one after another, beginning with the oldest. The woman was left alone. Jesus stood up and spoke to her. "Woman, where are they? Does no one condemn you?"

"No one, Master."

"Neither do I," said Jesus. "Go on your way. From now on, don't sin."]

John 9:1-3

Walking down the street, Jesus saw a man blind from birth. His disciples asked, "Rabbi, who sinned: this man or his parents, causing him to be born blind?"

Jesus said, "You're asking the wrong question. You're looking for someone to blame. There is no such cause-effect here. Look instead for what God can do.

Romans 6:6-11

Could it be any clearer? Our old way of life was nailed to the cross with Christ, a decisive end to that sin-miserable life—no longer captive to sin's demand! What we believe is this: If we get included in Christ's sin-conquering death, we also get included in his life-saving resurrection. We know that when Jesus was raised from the dead it was a signal of the end of death-as-the-end. Never again will death have the last word. When Jesus died, he took sin down with him, but alive he brings God down to us. From now on, think of it this way: Sin speaks a dead language that means nothing to you; God speaks your mother tongue, and you hang on every word. You are dead to sin and alive to God. That's what Jesus did.

I Corinthians 6:16-20

There's more to sex than mere skin on skin. Sex is as much spiritual mystery as physical fact. As written in Scripture, "The two become one." Since we want to become spiritually one with the Master, we must not pursue the kind of sex that avoids commitment and intimacy, leaving us more lonely than ever—the kind of sex that can never "become one." There is a sense in which sexual sins are different from all others. In sexual sin we violate the sacredness of our own bodies, these bodies that were made for God-given and God-modeled love, for "becoming one" with another. Or didn't you realize that your body is a sacred place, the place of the Holy Spirit? Don't you see that you can't live however you please, squandering what God paid such a high price for? The physical part of you is not some piece of property belonging to the spiritual part of you. God owns the whole works. So let people see God in and through your body.

Colossians 2:13b-15

Think of it! All sins forgiven, the slate wiped clean, that old arrest warrant canceled and nailed to Christ's cross. He stripped all the spiritual tyrants in the universe of their sham authority at the Cross and marched them naked through the streets.

Hebrews 8:10-12

This new plan I'm making with Israel isn't going to be written on paper, isn't going to be chiseled in stone; This time I'm writing out the plan *in* them, carving it on the lining of their hearts. I'll be their God, they'll be my people. They won't go to school to learn about me, or buy a book called *God in Five Easy Lessons*. They'll all get to know me firsthand, the little and the big, the small and the great. They'll get to know me by being kindly forgiven, with the slate of their sins forever wiped clean.

Hebrews 10:18-22

Once sins are taken care of for good, there's no longer any need to offer sacrifices for them. So, friends, we can now—without hesitation—walk right up to God, into "the Holy Place." Jesus has cleared the way by the blood of his sacrifice, acting as our priest before God. The "curtain" into God's presence is his body. So let's *do* it—full of belief, confident that we're presentable inside and out.

Hebrews 13:4

Honor marriage, and guard the sacredness of sexual intimacy between wife and husband. God draws a firm line against casual and illicit sex.

I John 1:8-10

If we claim that we're free of sin, we're only fooling ourselves. A claim like that is errant nonsense. On the other hand, if we admit our sins—simply come clean about them—he won't let us down; he'll be true to himself. He'll forgive our sins and purge us of all wrongdoing. If we claim that we've never sinned, we out-and-out contradict God—make a liar out of him. A claim like that only shows off our ignorance of God.

I John 3:18-24

My dear children, let's not just talk about love; let's practice real love. This is the only way we'll know we're living truly, living in God's reality. It's also the way to shut down debilitating self-criticism, even when there is something to it. For God is greater than our worried hearts and knows more about us than we do ourselves. And friends, once that's taken care of and we're no longer accusing or condemning ourselves, we're bold and free before God! We're able to stretch our hands out and receive what we asked for because we're doing what he said, doing what pleases him. Again, this is God's command: to believe in his personally named Son, Jesus Christ. He told us to love each other, in line with the original command. As we keep his commands, we live deeply and surely in him, and he lives in us. And this is how we experience his deep and abiding presence in us: by the Spirit he gave us.

DOUBTFUL? CONSIDER:

Exodus 6:30–7:1a

And Moses answered, "Look at me. I stutter. Why would Pharaoh listen to me?"
God told Moses, "Look at me.

Psalm 22:24

He has never let you down, never looked the other way when you were being kicked around. He has never wandered off to do his own thing; he has been right there, listening.

Isaiah 42:16

But I'll take the hand of those who don't know the way, who can't see where they're going. I'll be a personal guide to them, directing them through unknown country. I'll be right there to show them what roads to take, make sure they don't fall into the ditch. These are the things I'll be doing for them—sticking with them, not leaving them for a minute."

Isaiah 56:1-8

God's Message: "Guard my common good: Do what's right and do it in the right way, For salvation is just around the corner, my setting-things-right is about to go into action. How fortunate are you who enter into these things, you men and women who embrace them, Who keep Sabbath and don't defile it, who watch your step and don't do anything evil! Make sure no outsider who now follows God ever has occasion to say, 'God put me in second-class. I don't really belong.' And make sure no physically mutilated person is ever made to think, 'I'm damaged goods. I don't really belong.' " For God says: "To the mutilated who keep my Sabbaths and choose what delights me and keep a firm grip on my covenant, I'll provide them an honored place in my family and within my city, even more honored than that of sons and daughters. I'll confer permanent honors on them that will never be revoked. "And as for the outsiders who now follow me, working for me, loving my name, and wanting to be my servants—All who keep Sabbath and don't defile it, holding fast to my covenant—I'll bring them to my holy mountain and give them joy in my house of prayer. They'll be welcome to worship the same as the 'insiders,' to bring burnt offerings and sacrifices to my altar. Oh yes, my house of worship will be known as a house of prayer for all people." The Decree of the Master, God himself, who gathers in the exiles of Israel: "I will gather others also, gather them in with those already gathered."

Jeremiah 31:21-22

"Set up signposts to mark your trip home. Get a good map. Study the road conditions. The road out is the road back. Come back, dear virgin Israel, come back to your hometowns. How long will you flit here and there, indecisive? How long before you make up your fickle mind? God will create a new thing in this land: A transformed woman will embrace the transforming God!"

Jeremiah 33:2-3

"This is God's Message, the God who made earth, made it livable and lasting, known everywhere as God: 'Call to me and I will answer you. I'll tell you marvelous and wondrous things that you could never figure out on your own.'

Matthew 5:10-12

"You're blessed when your commitment to God provokes persecution. The persecution drives you even deeper into God's kingdom. "Not only that—count yourselves blessed every time people put you down or throw you out or speak lies about you to discredit me. What it means is that the truth is too close for comfort and they are uncomfortable. You can be glad when that happens—give a cheer, even!—for though they don't like it, *I* do! And all heaven applauds. And know that you are in good company. My prophets and witnesses have always gotten into this kind of trouble.

Mark 5:34

Jesus said to her, "Daughter, you took a risk of faith, and now you're healed and whole. Live well, live blessed! Be healed of your plague."

Romans 1:4-6

his unique identity as Son of God was shown by the Spirit when Jesus was raised from the dead, setting him apart as the Messiah, our Master. Through him we received both the generous gift of his life and the urgent task of passing it on to others who receive it by entering into obedient trust in Jesus. You are who you are through this gift and call of Jesus Christ!

Romans 6:12-14

That means you must not give sin a vote in the way you conduct your lives. Don't give it the time of day. Don't even run little errands that are connected with that old way of life. Throw yourselves wholeheartedly and full-time—remember, you've been raised from the dead!—into God's way of doing things. Sin can't tell you how to live. After all, you're not living under that old tyranny any longer. You're living in the freedom of God.

Romans 8:29-39

God knew what he was doing from the very beginning. He decided from the outset to shape the lives of those who love him along the same lines as the life of his Son. The Son stands first in the line of humanity he restored. We see the original and intended shape of our lives there in him. After God made that decision of what his children should be like, he followed it up by calling people by name. After he called them by name, he set them on a solid basis with himself. And then, after getting them established, he stayed with them to the end, gloriously completing what he had begun. So, what do you think? With God on our side like this, how can we lose? If God didn't hesitate to put everything on the line for us, embracing our condition and exposing himself to the worst by sending his own Son, is there anything else he wouldn't gladly and freely do for us? And who would dare tangle with God by messing with one of God's chosen? Who would dare even to point a finger? The One who died for us—who raised to life for us!—is in the presence of God at this very moment sticking up for us. Do you think anyone is going to be able to drive a wedge between us and Christ's love for us? There is no way! Not trouble, not hard times, not hatred, not hunger, not homelessness, not bullying threats, not backstabbing, not even the worst sins listed in Scripture: They kill us in cold blood because they hate you. We're sitting ducks; they pick us off one by one. None of this fazes us because Jesus loves us. I'm absolutely convinced that nothing—nothing living or dead, angelic or demonic, today or tomorrow, high or low, thinkable or unthinkable—absolutely *nothing* can get between us and God's love because of the way that Jesus our Master has embraced us.

Romans 10:8-10

So what exactly was Moses saying? The word that saves is right here, as near as the tongue in your mouth, as close as the heart in your chest. It's the word of faith that welcomes God to go to work and set things right for us. This is the core of our preaching. Say the welcoming word to God—"Jesus is my Master"—embracing, body and soul, God's work of doing in us what he did in raising Jesus from the dead. That's it. You're not "doing" anything; you're simply calling out to God, trusting him to do it for you. That's salvation. With your whole being you embrace God setting things right, and then you say it, right out loud: "God has set everything right between him and me!"

Romans 15:1b-3

Strength is for service, not status. Each one of us needs to look after the good of the people around us, asking ourselves, "How can I help?" That's exactly what Jesus did. He didn't make it easy for himself by avoiding people's troubles, but waded right in and helped out. "I took on the troubles of the troubled," is the way Scripture puts it.

2 Corinthians 5:4-5

Compared to what's coming, living conditions around here seem like a stopover in an unfurnished shack and we're tired of it! We've been giving a glimpse of the real thing, our true home, our resurrection bodies! The Spirit of God whets our appetite by giving us a taste of what's ahead. He puts a little of heaven in our hearts so that we'll never settle for less.

Ephesians 2:1-10

It wasn't so long ago that you were mired in that old stagnant life of sin. You let the world, which doesn't know the first thing about living, tell you how to live. You filled your lungs with polluted unbelief, and then exhaled disobedience. We all did it, all of us doing what we felt like doing, when we felt like doing it, all of us in the same boat. It's a wonder God didn't lose his temper and do away with the whole lot of us. Instead, immense in mercy and with an incredible love, he embraced us. He took our sin-dead lives and made us alive in Christ. He did all this on his own, with no help from us! Then he picked us up and set us down in highest heaven in company with Jesus, our Messiah. Now God has us where he wants us, with all the time in this world and the next to shower grace and kindness upon us in Christ Jesus. Saving is all his idea, and all his work. All we do is trust him enough to let him do it. It's God's gift from start to finish! We don't play the major role. If we did, we'd probably go around bragging that we'd done the whole thing! No, we neither make nor save ourselves. God does both the making and saving. He creates each of us by Christ Jesus to join him in the work he does, the good work he has gotten ready for us to do, work we had better be doing.

Titus 3:3-8

It wasn't so long ago that we ourselves were stupid and stubborn, easy marks for sin, ordered every which way by our glands, going around with a chip on our shoulder, hated and hating back. But when God, our kind and loving Savior God, stepped in, he saved us from all that. It was all his doing; we had nothing to do with it. He gave us a good bath, and we came out of it new people, washed inside and out by the Holy Spirit. Our Savior Jesus poured out new life so generously. God's gift has restored our relationship with him and given us back our lives. And there's more life to come—an eternity of life! You can count on this.

Hebrews 4:14-16

Now that we know what we have—Jesus, this great High Priest with ready access to God—let's not let it slip through our fingers. We don't have a priest who is out of touch with our reality. He's been through weakness and testing, experienced it all—all but the sin. So let's walk right up to him and get what he is so ready to give. Take the mercy, accept the help.

Hebrews 11:1

The fundamental fact of existence is that this trust in God, this faith, is the firm foundation under everything that makes life worth living. It's our handle on what we can't see.

James 4:7-10

So let God work his will in you. Yell a loud *no* to the Devil and watch him scarce. Say a quiet *yes* to God and he'll be there in no time. Quit dabbling in sin. Purify your inner life. Quit playing the field. Hit bottom, and cry your eyes out. The fun and games are over. Get serious, really serious. Get down on your knees before the Master; it's the only way you'll get on your feet.

I John 2:26-27

I've written to warn you about those who are trying to deceive you. But they're no match for what is embedded deeply within you—Christ's anointing, no less! You don't need any of their so-called teaching. Christ's anointing teaches you the truth on everything you need to know about yourself and him, uncontaminated by a single lie. Live deeply in what you were taught.

I John 3:4-8

All who indulge in a sinful life are dangerously lawless, for sin is a major disruption of God's order. Surely you know that Christ showed up in order to get rid of sin. There is no sin in him, and sin is not part of his program. No one who lives deeply in Christ makes a practice of sin. None of those who do practice sin have taken a good look at Christ. They've got him all backward. So, my dear children, don't let anyone divert you from the truth. It's the person who *acts* right who *is* right, just as we see it lived out in our righteous Messiah. Those who make a practice of sin are straight from the Devil, the pioneer in the practice of sin. The Son of God entered the scene to abolish the Devil's ways.

HOPELESS? CLING TO:

Psalm 34:17-18

Is anyone crying for help? God is listening, ready to rescue you. If your heart is broken, you'll find God right there; if you're kicked in the gut, he'll help you catch your breath.

Psalm 94:12-15

How blessed the man you train, God, the woman you instruct in your Word, Providing a circle of quiet within the clamor of evil, while a jail is being built for the wicked. God will never walk away from his people, never desert his precious people. Rest assured that justice is on its way and every good heart put right.

Psalm 116:1-8

I love God because he listened to me, listened as I begged for mercy. He listened so intently as I laid out my case before him.

Death stared me in the face, hell was hard on my heels. Up against it, I didn't know which way to turn; then I called out to God for help: "Please, God!" I cried out. "Save my life!" God is gracious—it is he who makes things right, our most compassionate God.

God takes the side of the helpless; when I was at the end of my rope, he saved me. I said to myself, "Relax and rest. God has showered you with blessings. Soul, you've been rescued from death; Eye, you've been rescued from tears; And you, Foot, were kept from stumbling."

Jeremiah 29:12-14

"When you call on me, when you come and pray to me, I'll listen. "When you come looking for me, you'll find me. "Yes, when you get serious about finding me and want it more than anything else, I'll make sure you won't be disappointed." God's Decree.

Jeremiah 33:10-11

"Yes, God's Message: 'You're going to look at this place, these empty and desolate towns of Judah and streets of Jerusalem, and say, "A wasteland. Unlivable. Not even a dog could live here." But time is coming when you're going to hear laughter and celebration, marriage festivities, people exclaiming, "Thank God-of-the-Angel-Armies. He's so good! His love never quits," as they bring thank offerings into God's Temple. I'll restore everything that was lost in this land. I'll make everything as good as new.' I, God say so.

Lamentations 3:19-23

I'll never forget the trouble, the utter lostness, the taste of ashes, the poison I've swallowed. I remember it all—oh, how well I remember—the feeling of hitting the bottom. But there's one other thing I remember, and remembering, I keep a grip on hope: God's loyal love couldn't have run out, his merciful love couldn't have dried up. They're created new every morning. How great your faithfulness!

Matthew 17:20

"Because you're not yet taking *God* seriously," said Jesus. "The simple truth is that if you had a mere kernel of faith, a poppy seed, say, you would tell this mountain, 'Move!' and it would move. There is nothing you wouldn't be able to tackle."

Luke 6:20-21

Then he spoke: You're blessed when you've lost it all. God's kingdom is there for the finding. You're blessed when you're ravenously hungry. Then you're ready for the Messianic meal. You're blessed when the tears flow freely. Joy comes with the morning.

John 16:33

I've told you all this so that trusting me, you will be unshakable and assured, deeply at peace. In this godless world you will continue to experience difficulties. But take heart! I've conquered the world."

Acts 3:16

Faith in Jesus' name put this man, whose condition you know so well, on his feet—yes, faith and nothing but faith put this man healed and whole right before your eyes.

Acts 10:34-36

Peter fairly exploded with his good news: "It's God's own truth, nothing could be plainer: God plays no favorites! It makes no difference who you are or where you're from—if you want God and are ready to do as he says, the door is open. The Message he sent to the children of Israel—that through Jesus Christ everything is being put together again—well, he's doing it everywhere, among everyone.

Romans 4:19-24

Abraham didn't focus on his own impotence and say, "It's hopeless. This hundred-year-old body could never father a child." Nor did he survey Sarah's decades of infertility and give up. He didn't tiptoe around God's promise asking cautiously skeptical questions. He plunged into the promise and came up strong, ready for God, sure that God would make good on what he had said. That's why it is said, "Abraham was declared fit before God by trusting God to set him right." But it's not just Abraham; it's also us! The same thing gets said about us when we embrace and believe the One who brought Jesus to life when the conditions were equally hopeless.

Romans 6:19-23

I'm using this freedom language because it's easy to picture. You can readily recall, can't you, how at one time the more you did just what you felt like doing—not caring about others, not caring about God—the worse your life became and the less freedom you had? And how much different is it now as you live in God's freedom, your lives healed and expansive in holiness? As long as you did what you felt like doing, ignoring God, you didn't have to bother with right thinking or right living, or right *anything* for that matter. But do you call that a free life? What did you get out of it? Nothing you're proud of now. Where did it get you? A dead end. But now that you've found you don't have to listen to sin tell you what to do, and have discovered the delight of listening to God telling you, what a surprise! A whole, healed, put-together life right now, with more and more of life on the way! Work hard for sin your whole life and your pension is death. But God's gift is *real life*, eternal life, delivered by Jesus, our Master.

Romans 7:24-25

I've tried everything and nothing helps. I'm at the end of my rope. Is there no one who can do anything for me? Isn't that the real question? The answer, thank God, is that Jesus Christ can and does. He acted to set things right in this life of contradictions where I want to serve God with all my heart and mind, but am pulled by the influence of sin to do something totally different.

Romans 8:10-14

But for you who welcome him, in whom he dwells—even though you still experience all the limitations of sin—you yourself experience life on God's terms. It stands to reason, doesn't it, that if the alive-and-present God who raised Jesus from the dead moves into your life, he'll do the same thing in you that he did in Jesus, bringing you alive to himself? When God lives and breathes in you (and he does, as surely as he did in Jesus), you are delivered from that dead life. With his Spirit living in you, your body will be as alive as Christ's! So don't you see that we don't owe this old do-it-yourself life one red cent. There's nothing in it for us, nothing at all. The best thing to do is give it a decent burial and get on with your new life. God's Spirit beckons. There are things to do and places to go!

Romans 8:22-28

All around us we observe a pregnant creation. The difficult times of pain throughout the world are simply birth pangs. But it's not only around us; it's *within* us. The Spirit of God is arousing us within. We're also feeling the birth pangs. These sterile and barren bodies of ours are yearning for full deliverance. That is why waiting does not diminish us, any more than waiting diminishes a pregnant mother. We are enlarged in the waiting. We, of course, don't see what is enlarging us. But the longer we wait, the larger we become, and the more joyful our expectancy. Meanwhile, the moment we get tired in the waiting, God's Spirit is right alongside helping us along. If we don't know how or what to pray, it doesn't matter. He does our praying in and for us, making prayer out of our wordless sighs, our aching groans. He knows us far better than we know ourselves, knows our pregnant condition, and keeps us present before God. That's why we can be so sure that every detail in our lives of love for God is worked into something good.

I Corinthians 2:9

That's why we have this Scripture text: No one's ever seen or heard anything like this, Never so much as imagined anything quite like it—What God has arranged for those who love him.

Ephesians 3:20

God can do anything, you know—far more than you could ever imagine or guess or request in your wildest dreams! He does it not by pushing us around but by working within us, his Spirit deeply and gently within us.

2 Thessalonians 1:5-10

All this trouble is a clear sign that God has decided to make you fit for the kingdom. You're suffering now, but justice is on the way. When the Master Jesus appears out of heaven in a blaze of fire with his strong angels, he'll even up the score by settling accounts with those who gave you such a bad time. His coming will be the break we've been waiting for. Those who refuse to know God and refuse to obey the Message will pay for what they've done. Eternal exile from the presence of the Master and his splendid power is their sentence. But on that very same day when he comes, he will be exalted by his followers and celebrated by all who believe—and all because you believed what we told you.

Revelation 21:3-5

I heard a voice thunder from the Throne: "Look! Look! God has moved into the neighborhood, making his home with men and women! They're his people, he's their God. He'll wipe every tear from their eyes. Death is gone for good—tears gone, crying gone, pain gone—all the first order of things gone." The Enthroned continued, "Look! I'm making everything new. Write it all down—each word dependable and accurate."

FEARFUL? TAKE TO HEART:

Deuteronomy 31:8

God is striding ahead of you. He's right there with you. He won't let you down; he won't leave you. Don't be intimidated. Don't worry."

Joshua 1:9

Haven't I commanded you? Strength! Courage! Don't be timid; don't get discouraged. God, your God, is with you every step you take."

Psalm 91:1-16

You who sit down in the High God's presence, spend the night in Shaddai's shadow, Say this: "God, you're my refuge. I trust in you and I'm safe!" That's right—he rescues you from hidden traps, shields you from deadly hazards. His huge outstretched arms protect you—under them you're perfectly safe; his arms fend off all harm. Fear nothing—not wild wolves in the night, not flying arrows in the day, Not disease that prowls through the darkness, not disaster that erupts at high noon. Even though others succumb all around, drop like flies right and left, no harm will even graze you. You'll stand untouched, watch it all from a distance, watch the wicked turn into corpses. Yes, because God's your refuge, the High God your very own home, Evil can't get close to you, harm can't get through the door. He ordered his angels to guard you wherever you go. If you stumble, they'll catch you; their job is to keep you from falling. You'll walk unharmed among lions and snakes, and kick young lions and serpents from the path. "If you'll hold on to me for dear life," says God, "I'll get you out of any trouble. I'll give you the best of care if you'll only get to know and trust me. Call me and I'll answer, be at your side in bad times; I'll rescue you, then throw you a party. I'll give you a long life, give you a long drink of salvation!"

Psalm 121:1-8

I look up to the mountains; does my strength come from mountains? No, my strength comes from God, who made heaven, and earth, and mountains. He won't let you stumble, your Guardian God won't fall asleep. Not on your life! Israel's Guardian will never doze or sleep. God's your Guardian, right at your side to protect you—Shielding you from sunstroke, sheltering you from moonstroke. God guards you from every evil, he guards your very life. He guards you when you leave and when you return, he guards you now, he guards you always.

Isaiah 43:1b-3

"Don't be afraid, I've redeemed you. I've called your name. You're mine. When you're in over your head, I'll be there with you. When you're in rough waters, you will not go down. When you're between a rock and a hard place, it won't be a dead end—Because I am God, your personal God, The Holy of Israel, your Savior.

Isaiah 49:9

I tell prisoners, 'Come on out. You're free!' and those huddled in fear, 'It's all right. It's safe now.'

Isaiah 54:14-17

You'll be built solid, grounded in righteousness, far from any trouble—nothing to fear! far from terror—it won't even come close! If anyone attacks you, don't for a moment suppose that I sent them, And if any should attack, nothing will come of it. I create the blacksmith who fires up his forge and makes a weapon designed to kill. I also create the destroyer—but no weapon that can hurt you has ever been forged. Any accuser who takes you to court will be dismissed as a liar. This is what God's servants can expect. I'll see to it that everything works out for the best." God's Decree.

Luke 19:26

"He said, 'That's what I mean: Risk your life and get more than you ever dreamed of. Play it safe and end up holding the bag.

John 12:24-25

"Listen carefully: Unless a grain of wheat is buried in the ground, dead to the world, it is never any more than a grain of wheat. But if it is buried, it sprouts and reproduces itself many times over. In the same way, anyone who holds on to life just as it is destroys that life. But if you let it go, reckless in your love, you'll have it forever, real and eternal.

John 14:25-27

"I'm telling you these things while I'm still living with you. The Friend, the Holy Spirit whom the Father will send at my request, will make everything plain to you. He will remind you of all the things I have told you. I'm leaving you well and whole. That's my parting gift to you. Peace. I don't leave you the way you're used to being left—feeling abandoned, bereft. So don't be upset. Don't be distraught.

I Corinthians 7:23-24

All of you, slave and free both, were once held hostage in a sinful society. Then a huge sum was paid out for your ransom. So please don't, out of old habit, slip back into being or doing what everyone else tells you. Friends, stay where you were called to be. God is there. Hold the high ground with him at your side.

Ephesians 6:10-18

And that about wraps it up. God is strong, and he wants you strong. So take everything the Master has set out for you, well-made weapons of the best materials. And put them to use so you will be able to stand up to everything the Devil throws your way. This is no weekend war that we'll walk away from and forget about in a couple of hours. This is for keeps, a life-or-death fight to the finish against the Devil and all his angels. Be prepared. You're up against far more than you can handle on your own. Take all the help you can get, every weapon God has issued, so that when it's all over but the shouting you'll still be on your feet. Truth, righteousness, peace, faith, and salvation are more than words. Learn how to apply them. You'll need them throughout your life. God's Word is an *indispensable* weapon. In the same way, prayer is essential in this ongoing warfare. Pray hard and long. Pray for your brothers and sisters. Keep your eyes open. Keep each other's spirits up so that no one falls behind or drops out.

Philippians 4:6-7

Don't fret or worry. Instead of worrying, pray. Let petitions and praises shape your worries into prayers, letting God know your concerns. Before you know it, a sense of God's wholeness, everything coming together for good, will come and settle you down. It's wonderful what happens when Christ displaces worry at the center of your life.

Hebrews 6:18-20

We who have run for our very lives to God have every reason to grab the promised hope with both hands and never let go. It's an unbreakable spiritual lifeline, reaching past all appearances right to the very presence of God where Jesus, running on ahead of us, has taken up his permanent post as high priest for us, in the order of Melchizedek.

I John 4:4

My dear children, you come from God and belong to God. You have already won a big victory over those false teachers, for the Spirit in you is far stronger than anything in the world.

UNLOVED? CHERISH:

Psalm 18:16-24

But me he caught—reached all the way from sky to sea; he pulled me out Of that ocean of hate, that enemy chaos, the void in which I was drowning. They hit me when I was down, but God stuck by me. He stood me up on a wide-open field; I stood there saved—surprised to be loved! God made my life complete when I placed all the pieces before him. When I got my act together, he gave me a fresh start. Now I'm alert to

God's ways; I don't take God for granted. Every day I review the ways he works; I try not to miss a trick. I feel put back together, and I'm watching my step. God rewrote the text of my life when I opened the book of my heart to his eyes.

Psalm 56:8

You've kept track of my every toss and turn through the sleepless nights, Each tear entered in your ledger, each ache written in your book.

Isaiah 43:3-4

I paid a huge price for you: all of Egypt, with rich Cush and Seba thrown in! *That's* how much you mean to me! *That's* how much I love you! I'd sell off the whole world to get you back, trade the creation just for you.

Isaiah 54:10

For even if the mountains walk away and the hills fall to pieces, My love won't walk away from you, my covenant commitment of peace won't fall apart." The God who has compassion on you says so.

Jeremiah 31:3

God told them, "I've never quit loving you and never will. Expect love, love, and more love!

Acts 20:28

"Now it's up to you. Be on your toes—both for yourselves and your congregation of sheep. The Holy Spirit has put you in charge of these people—God's people they are—to guard and protect them. God himself thought they were worth dying for.

Romans 5:6-8

Christ arrives right on time to make this happen. He didn't, and doesn't, wait for us to get ready. He presented himself for this sacrificial death when we were far too weak and rebellious to do anything to get ourselves ready. And even if we hadn't been so weak, we wouldn't have known what to do anyway. We can understand someone dying for a person worth dying for, and we can understand how someone good and noble could inspire us to selfless sacrifice. But God put his love on the line for us by offering his Son in sacrificial death while we were of no use whatever to him.

I Corinthians 1:7-9

Just think—you don't need a thing, you've got it all! All God's gifts are right in front of you as you wait expectantly for our Master Jesus to arrive on the scene for the Finale. And not only that, but God himself is right alongside to keep you steady and on track until things are all wrapped up by Jesus. God, who got you started in this spiritual adventure, shares with us the life of his Son and our Master Jesus. He will never give up on you. Never forget that.

Ephesians 2:19-22

That's plain enough, isn't it? You're no longer wandering exiles. This kingdom of faith is now your home country. You're no longer strangers or outsiders. You *belong* here, with as much right to the name Christian as anyone. God is building a home. He's using us all—irrespective of how we got here—in what he is building. He used the apostles and prophets for the foundation. Now he's using you, fitting you in brick by brick, stone by stone, with Christ Jesus as the cornerstone that holds all the parts together. We see it taking shape day after day—a holy temple built by God, all of us built into it, a temple in which God is quite at home.

I Timothy 1:12-16

I'm so grateful to Christ Jesus for making me adequate to do this work. He went out on a limb, you know, in trusting me with this ministry. The only credentials I brought to it were violence and witch hunts and arrogance. But I was treated mercifully because I didn't know what I was doing—didn't know Who I was doing it against! Grace mixed with faith and love poured over me and into me. And all because of Jesus. Here's a word you can take to heart and depend on: Jesus Christ came into the world to save sinners. I'm proof—Public Sinner Number One—of someone who could never have made it apart from sheer mercy. And now he shows me off—evidence of his endless patience—to those who are right on the edge of trusting him forever.

I Peter 2:23-25

They called him every name in the book and he said nothing back. He suffered in silence, content to let God set things right. He used his servant body to carry our sins to the Cross so we could be rid of sin, free to live the right way. His wounds became your healing. You were lost sheep with no idea who you were or where you were going. Now you're named and kept for good by the Shepherd of your souls.

HELLO, CONFLICT. MEET PLOT TWIST:

REFLECTIONS FOR DIGGING IN AND PRESSING ON

CHAPTER 1:

1. How would you define sex? Has your definition changed over time?

2. What part did others (family, friends, peers, role models, partners) play in shaping your view or definition of sex?

3. What story or stories brought you to this point in your life and this book?

4. Do you relate better to choices being taken or given? Or are you able to understand both cases?

5. How would you complete the sentence, "If only...?"

6. Have you ever found a "piece of the puzzle" you had previously missed or forgotten?

7. Can you name/identify the pain in your life? If not, are you willing to take some time to contemplate your experience(s) to name it (them)?

8. Retracing detrimental times can dredge up buried pain and stir up fresh regret as we replay the unpleasant

scenes in our minds. However, are you willing to revisit your memories at least one more time, either on your own or with professional help as necessary? (A list of possible resources is available on page 137.) Instead of rerunning the stories to see, hear, or feel the familiar parts, can you try to dig past the glaring to reveal the less conspicuous? Try to detect if you might have missed or forgotten any facts or pieces that would shed a different light on your memories.

CHAPTER 2:

1. Have you ever considered that truth could be tangible or intangible?

2. Does your life story encourage questions or doubts about God to linger in your mind?

3. What is your life's motivating force—your number one goal, desire, dream, or wish? If the question stumps you, try saying, "If I could have anything, it would be (fill in the blank)."

4. Was the truth ever beyond your ability to accept? If so, what truth concoctions did you create to survive?

5. What have you concluded about your worth—how do you view yourself?

6. Recalling the Belief → Feeling → Action pattern, can you spot any untruthful beliefs influencing your feelings and actions? Any areas where the familiar more than the factual guides you? If so, where have these misleading beliefs steered the places, situations, or consequences in your life?

7. Has an inability to justify or understand another person's actions led to frustration?

8. Continue to locate where crafty lies have sabotaged truth in your life with distortion or confusion.

CHAPTER 3:

1. Has either your physical or emotional eyesight ever misled you?

2. Do you recognize a disparity or gap between where you are and where you want to be?

3. "True Love Waits" is one saying. If you had to coin a phrase about love, what would it be? Any thoughts are fair game!

4. Unity, commitment, and fulfillment are all intended components of sex. Have you experienced any of these ideals?

5. Do you have a tale of driving amidst chaos or bedlam? How do you feel about placing confines or limitations on life or sex? Are there any areas where you need to install bumper guards? If so, would these bumpers resemble rules, accountability, boundaries, or something else?

6. Have you found several ways that "will not work?" If you had choices, how can your previous decisions make you wiser?

7. Have you been grasping, stretching, or leaping to attain your desires? If so, has reckless living ended in reckless results? Has a good desire crossed the line and transformed into greed or disregard?

8. Have you become aware that fear or pain is controlling areas of your life? Do you think your capability to love or trust has diminished or disappeared?

9. Can you identify emotional walls you have built, hoping to protect yourself?

10. Do you notice any faults within your blueprints for life? If so, will you start flipping your previous ways and thoughts?

CHAPTER 4:

1. Has "light" entered a dark place of your life that once caused you to stumble or hide? Have you glimpsed sin's flimsy framework of lies? If so, has sin lost some of its enticement?

2. If you desire to leave the darkness, you cannot continue to live the same way. Separation is necessary to distinguish "what was" from "what is" or "what will be." Looking forward, can you name one way your patterns, beliefs, or actions could separate themselves from your previous ways?

3. God deemed the vegetation in the Creation story good, but not because of its specific growth spot—*not* because of its circumstances. The vegetation blossomed because of its connection to a life source. Are you connected to a source of life and truth? If not, where could you find such a source?

4. The fruit of the Spirit is love, joy, peace, patience, kindness, goodness, faithfulness, gentleness, and self-control. Which fruit do you lack most in your life?

5. Have you ever been accustomed to the darkness of loneliness, confusion, or sadness? Can you pick out what served as the right light for your need and how the light addressed your darkness with both pinpoint accuracy and gentle respect?

6. Do you have a sense of community, either with one person or with multiple people? Is community a hard thing for you to do or imagine? Can you think of any instance in which unity or variety made a good impression on you?

7. God still asks us to be productive and prosperous. Have you recognized natural inclinations or talents that you can strengthen or develop? Can you spy any areas of abundance in your life that have room to grow and bless someone else?

8. To which people or causes are you most drawn? What restoration would you like to help create in the world—what good would you like to see?

CHAPTER 5:

1. Sin often causes us to hide or place blame elsewhere. Have you sensed God seeking you though you have tried to run or hide? Where are you inclined to attribute blame?

2. Sin attempts to find a substitute for God and His ways through our own desires and efforts. What substitutions have you chased after instead of God?

3. Sin will always result in negative or painful consequences. Can you determine a time when sin preceded an unwelcome outcome in your life?

4. Embarrassment and shame are encouraged by our enemy, not God. Do you feel attacked or plagued by either of these feelings? Has embarrassment or shame changed your opinion of yourself or your future?

5. God never runs out of options, and He offers countless chances. Have you experienced either of these truths

before? Or are you struggling to get one, or both, of them to sink in?

6. How different would your life be if you allowed yourself to accept grace by taking advantage of a second (or third or more) chance?

7. When considering the four sin results that surfaced from the Creation story, which sin result causes you the most difficulty? Which antidote to sin do you find the most surprising or transforming?

8. God still addresses Satan first when responding to sin. How could you address Satan first in your current battle?

9. Did you ever know there is *joy* in heaven when *one* sinner admits to accepting sin's bait but desires help to refuse its continued lure? How do you envision heaven's celebration?

CHAPTER 6:

1. What are the best words of wisdom someone has ever spoken to you? Feel free to define "wisdom" in either a genuine or a sarcastic sense, depending on your experience!

2. Has time healed your pain or caused your pain to fester, grow, or spread?

3. Has your view of God ever changed, for the better or worse, after receiving advice or criticism?

4. What would you list as the troubles you can't get a handle on?

5. Have you ever suffered a just consequence because of a dumb move on your part? Have you endured

a problem, though, because of an unjust situation?
Which was harder to deal with: the hurt caused by
your own doing or the hurt caused by someone else?

6. Do you struggle with an inclination to diagnose or
   pass judgment on others' problems too quickly?

7. Have you ever longed for a quick fix to help you get by?
   Have you ever asked God, "Why?" Or did you believe
   that God wouldn't welcome or allow your questions?

8. Can you remember a time when you had joy in the
   face of pain? Peace amid suffering?

9. What master's level lesson have you learned in Pain's
   classroom? Has this lesson steered you to empathy or
   bitterness?

10. During a time of pain, would you find it helpful to
    explore how Jesus had a similar experience to what
    you are walking through?

11. If you were to subject your heart to a litmus test, what
    would the results indicate as your heart's condition?

12. Whom do you perceive as being the ultimately offended
    one: yourself or God? If you ever considered forgiving
    or praying for the person(s) who mistreated you, did
    you believe you would need to accept, condone, or
    "get over" their actions first? Have you attributed the
    breaking, harming, or wounding work of sin to love
    by mistake?

13. Has unforgiveness caused you to relive pain on repeat?
    Have you imagined that a scenario could undo or
    make up for your experiences? God's emphasis on our
    need to forgive actually equates to the emphasis that
    He places on our need to heal: Would you have ever

guessed that forgiveness could be to *your* advantage when trying to heal?

14. If you identify sin as the source of your pain, how does that change the entire trajectory of your healing journey or your ability to entertain forgiveness?

15. What has abuse or regrettable decisions robbed from you that you would like God to restore?

CHAPTER 7:

1. Have you ever quit something? Was it a funny, celebrated, or not-so-funny experience?

2. To what extent has sexual brokenness spread in your soul? Does your heart or mind bear hidden mutations?

3. You are at a crossroads. You can continue in the same direction or try a new way. If you want to avoid more of what you have already experienced, what could be your first step toward quitting a previous habit or mindset?

4. Do you typically prefer the destination or the journey? If you've ever had to navigate without prior experience, a map, or an app to assist you, how'd that go for you?

5. Do you view God's will as elusive or flexible? Do you believe you have options to transform the canvas of your life—to move the mountains that have crowded your canvas or turn a blob into something better? If not, what do you hear the nagging voice of the enemy whispering to discourage you?

6. Thinking about Rahab's story, we might never see the complete picture of how our choices affect the future. Yet, given their power to perchance equal life or death for yourself or others, do you possess a more

profound regard for your choices? Have you already spotted proof of this fact in the present?

7. We also learned the story of Hagar, who was pregnant, alone, and on the run. Can you sympathize with any or all of Hagar's experiences? What would it mean for you to know that God *sees* you?

8. What label(s) have you given to yourself? What label(s) have others tried to assign you?

9. Which of Jesus' admonishments to the Pharisees did you find most humorous?

10. Though it might not be the letter of the law, do you prioritize anything over showing kindness? Or does something obstruct your willingness to care for others?

11. "Let any one of you who is without sin be the first to throw a stone at her" (John 8:7). Can you imagine how this sentence could dispel your accusers' or critics' superiority? Who is your loudest critic: someone else or yourself?

12. Which has been a higher priority for you: undoing your past or redeeming your future?

13. Do you consider God willing and unafraid to enter *any* situation? Can you name anything He cannot redeem, heal, resurrect, transform, or restore? If, instead, your hurt arises from pieces that were absent, lacking, defective, or screwed up, can you name any reason not to anticipate or accept His supplementation as He sees fit to supply?

14. Which of the two verses below gives you the most comfort or hope?

"It is not the healthy who need a doctor, but the sick. I have not come to call the righteous, but sinners" (Mark 2:17).

"The thief comes only to steal and kill and destroy; I have come that they may have life, and have it to the full" (John 10:10).

15. Before truth can impact your heart or life, it must first translate into action. Were you willing to surrender your life to Jesus—either for the first time or for a fresh start? If so, would you be open to sharing this momentous step with someone who could encourage you on your journey? But first, can you hear it? That's heaven's celebration *for you*! Enjoy the sound!

CHAPTER 8:

1. Can you recall something in which you invested extensive preparations or planning but has since faded in importance or value to you? In what ways have you chosen the "fleeting" over the "forever?"

2. Every person bears the stamp of God's image. What facets of God's personality and character do you reflect?

3. Thinking back to Gomer's story, when she hit rock bottom, she was naked, for sale, and held no other options. Can you literally or figuratively relate to any or all of Gomer's circumstances?

4. Which concept is harder to comprehend: God's shocking love or His undeserved grace?

5. Do you know someone who is living without the knowledge of her value?

6. We are often guilty of placing utmost importance on the dreams we identify solely through our earthly eyesight. How does an accurate perception of "forever" give us a better perspective on the "just now?"

7. Do you relate to the disciple Thomas, who needed proof before believing in the suffering Messiah? Do you feel that Jesus poses too high of a risk for disappointment?

8. Up close, life can look hopeless or give the impression evil has won. But from God's viewpoint, what could be His plan for your life?

9. Jesus left His grave clothes and the tomb behind Him, but He chose to carry out His scars. His scars provided the evidence that some needed before believing in His resurrection. Scars, whether visible or invisible, provide proof that we are acquainted with suffering, but they also advertise hope. What unique reassurance could your one-of-a-kind scars provide to someone else?

10. Jesus' scars also bridged the gap between His triumph and our suffering, so we could dare to believe that suffering sometimes paves the road to victory. Can you dare to think that victorious joy is still possible despite familiarity with suffering?

11. What are you willing to let pass through your scars?

12. When someone asks you how you pulled through, how will you answer?

13. Do you agree that we live in a world full of wounded hearts? Can you celebrate your rescue while neglecting to look behind for those who still need rescuing?

14. God has no issues deciphering a mess from an identity nor untangling imposed shame from innate worth. And He's added a twist to your life's story: You can now erase shame from its pages! However your life ending previously read, how does it read now? What purely wrong ending would you like Him to include in your story's rewrite?

15. Has God thrown you a curveball? Demolished your doubt? Or clobbered your shame? If so, will you join Him as He redefines "impossible" with "possible?"

ACKNOWLEDGMENTS

Dearest Savior, thank You for not giving up on me. Each day, I grow more assured that not a single day of my life has escaped Your watch or care. You have proven Yourself good and faithful time after time. May all my efforts be for Your glory alone, and may the evidence of Your Kingdom on Earth abound.

Jeff, thank you for your patience during my healing journey. I may not have logged the countless hours you spent listening to my hopeful plans and re-reading rough drafts, but I'm convinced heaven has kept track! Thank you for stretching your understanding of my experiences and never making light of my pain. I do not take your love, care, or trustworthiness for granted.

Alyssa, Madison, and Faith, thanks for being my sounding boards—I used to be cool, but now, I need your help! I could have never written this book without your generosity in creating space for me to work or your eagerness to dream right along with me. Your tenderness for hurting souls not only amazes me but it also sustains me. You are proof that love is always worth fighting for.

Gina, you have stuck with me for what seems like a lifetime. I can hardly recall a life experience without you in it. You were the first person with whom I felt comfortable sharing my messiness. If you hadn't responded in the manner you did, who knows where I would be today? Our friendship forms my backbone and is a rare guarantee in an otherwise unstable world. I love you dearly.

To my parents, thank you for letting me share my story and encouraging me to do so. I am who I am because you pointed me to Jesus early in my life. Mom, your prayers and support kept me going countless times, and your encouragement always arrived when I needed it the most.

To my late Grandpa Dancho, thanks to your life and hard work, I now hold my dream. I hope that through this book, others will be able to honor you with those exact words. And to my late Grandpa Overheidt, I'm still realizing your prayers for me and witnessing their answers. I miss you, but I can still hear your song. I know heaven is enjoying it.

NOTES

1 Cindy Boren, "Pro Surfer Mick Fanning Fights Off Terrifying Shark Attack," *The Washington Post*, July 20, 2015, https://www.washingtonpost.com/news/early-lead/wp/2015/07/19/pro-surfer-fights-off-shark-attack-during-competition-in-south-africa/.

2 "Goodbye Mom!" *Piffe.com*, accessed June 13, 2017, http://www.piffe.com/jokes/goodbye-mom.php .

3 "Crafty," *Merriam-Webster.com*, accessed January 24, 2021, https://www.merriam-webster.com/dictionary/crafty.

4 "Cunning," *Merriam-Webster.com,* accessed January 24, 2021, https://www.merriam-webster.com/dictionary/cunning.

5 "Samuel Johnson Quotes," *BrainyQuote.com,* accessed June 14, 2017, https://www.brainyquote.com/quotes/quotes/s/samuel-john378836.html.

6 "Thomas A. Edison Quotes," *BrainyQuote.com*, accessed July 24, 2020, https://www.brainyquote.com/quotes/thomas_a_edison_132683.

7 "Red Adair Quotes," *BrainyQuote.com,* accessed June 18, 2018, https://www.brainyquote.com/quotes/red_adair_195665.

8 "The Books of the Bible," *BlueLetterBible.org*, accessed June 19, 2018, https://www.blueletterbible.org/study/misc/66books.cfm.

9 "How Many Chapters In Each Book Of The Bible," *Thebible.life*, accessed June 24, 2020, https://thebible.life/bible-books-and-number-of-chapters/.

10 "Bob Ross > Quotes," *Goodreads.com*, accessed July 25, 2020, https://www.goodreads.com/author/quotes/102372.Bob_Ross.

11 "Bob Ross > Quotes," *Goodreads.com*, accessed July 25, 2020, https://www.goodreads.com/author/quotes/102372.Bob_Ross.

12 "Redeeming Gomer: The Price," *Timeintheword.org*, May 23, 2017, https://timeintheword.org/2017/05/23/redeeming-gomer-the-price/.

13 "National Coalition Against Domestic Violence > Resources," *NCADV.org*, accessed April 28, 2023, https://ncadv.org/RESOURCES.

14 "SAMHSA Substance Abuse and Mental Health Services Administration," *Samhsa.gov*, accessed May 28, 2023, https://www.samhsa.gov/#.

ABOUT THE AUTHOR

Laurel Burns suffered too long to let her healing go to waste. So she now works to redirect the narrative of sexual shame in women's private lives and the public realm because she is adamant that healing and transformation are possible for anyone suffering from any form of sexual shame. Sharing the insights she has gained through failure and success, Laurel hopes to spare one woman from the potential hazards and duration of this agonizing battle—*you*. When not taking a swing at shame, it's safe to guess that Laurel is cooking. However, now that her daughters are nearly grown, she might finally remember which way leads out of the kitchen. Perhaps. Until then, she relies on her favorite ingredients: coffee and music. Follow her on Instagram @laureljburns.

Printed in the USA
CPSIA information can be obtained
at www.ICGtesting.com
JSHW050309020224
56281JS00011B/164